Book-keeping ana Accounts for Hotel and Catering Studies

Grace Paige

Lecturer in Accounts, Costing and Control, Hastings College of Technology

Jane Paige

Lecturer in Commercial Subjects, Eastbourne College of Further Education

HOLT, RINEHART AND WINSTON
London · New York · Sydney · Toronto

Holt, Rinehart and Winston Ltd: 1 St Anne's Road, Eastbourne, East Sussex BN21 3UN.

British Library Cataloguing in Publication Data

Paige, Grace
    Book-keeping and accounts for hotel and catering
    studies.
    1.   Hotels, taverns, etc. – Great Britain – Accounting
    2.   Caterers and catering – Great Britain – Accounting
    I.   Title   II. Paige, Jane
    657'.837'00941   HF5686

ISBN 0-03-910425-7

Printed in Great Britain by
The Pitman Press, Bath

Last digit is print no: 9 8 7 6 5 4 3 2 1

Contents

5   The General Journal   66

6   The Tabular Ledger   76

7   Accounting for Wages   102

8   The Trial Balance   119

9   The Final Accounts   132

10   Reports and Statistics   146

Preface

With mechanization and microcomputers revolutionizing accounting procedures and office technology, recent textbooks have been directed and biased towards the more sophisticated approaches to accounting systems. Such books assume that students already have a knowledge of the double-entry book-keeping theory and tend to forget that figures on paper produced by computers require interpretation and an understanding of the system that compiles those figures.

It must also be remembered that a very high percentage of the hotel and catering industry is still made up of smaller establishments and hotels with fewer than 50 bedrooms, in which highly sophisticated computerized accounts systems would be neither warranted nor practical.

The aim of this textbook is to provide students with clear explanations, simple examples and ample exercises which will clearly underline the principles and theory of the double-entry book-keeping system. It is written primarily for students with no previous knowledge of accounts who are studying for the City and Guilds Book-keeping and Hotel Reception examinations, the City and Guilds General Catering courses, TEC certificates and diplomas and other ancillary catering courses. It should also prove useful to the small hotelier and caterer whose knowledge of accounts is limited.

With this basic knowledge of the double-entry book-keeping theory and principles students should be able to interpret, adapt and apply their knowledge to whatever sophisticated accounts system they are called upon to implement.

Grace Paige
Jane Paige

1 Introduction

Whenever a business is created its trading transactions must be recorded, first to provide a functional record and second to meet statutory requirements and taxation obligations. Book-keeping is the recording of the transactions of a business in a simple and reliable manner so that the business executive has a complete record which will reveal:

1. whether the business has made a profit or a loss;
2. how that profit or loss has been made;
3. the financial position of the business in terms of assets and liabilities.

1.1 THE DOUBLE-ENTRY SYSTEM

The double-entry book-keeping system (Fig. 1.1) is based on the principle that for every business transaction that takes place *two* entries must be made in the accounts: a debit entry (left-hand side of an account), showing goods or value coming into the business, and a corresponding credit entry (right-hand side of an account), showing goods or value going out of the business.

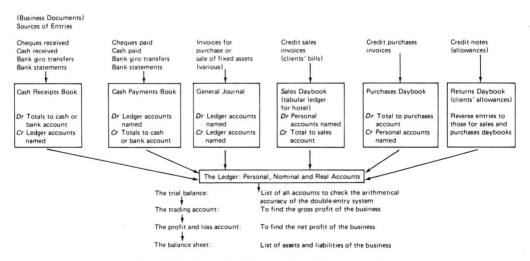

Figure 1.1 *The double-entry book-keeping system.*

Example 1

In a restaurant food and wine were purchased for which £10 in cash was paid. In this case the purchases account would be *debited* (left-hand side) with £10 for goods coming in and the cash account would be *credited* (right-hand side) with £10 cash going out as payment for the food and wine.

Example 2

Sales of food and drink as meals in a restaurant amounted to £20 cash. In this case the sales account would be *credited* (right-hand side) with the value of the food and drink leaving the restaurant as meals, and the cash account would be *debited* (left-hand side) with the £20 cash coming into the business from the sales.

Example 3

A restaurateur paid out £500 cash as wages to the members of his staff. In this case the cash account would be *credited* with the £500 going out of the business as wages and the wages account would be *debited* with £500, being the cost of labour used in the business.

Example 4

A hotelier sent a cheque for £300 as payment of her electricity bill. In this case the bank account would be *credited* with the £300 going out of the business and the electricity account would be *debited* with £300, being the cost of the electricity used in the business.

The whole of the double-entry system is based on this principle: that for every business transaction that takes place there must be *two* entries in the accounts − a debit entry (value in) and a corresponding credit entry (value out). It will follow from this principle that at any given time the total debit entries should equal the total credit entries, and it is therefore simple to make a check for arithmetical accuracy and locate errors. This is the main advantage of the system.

1.2   BUSINESS DOCUMENTS

Before one can understand book-keeping it is necessary to have a knowledge of the basic business documents that are used for control purposes and as the sources of entries for the accounts system. These documents can be any size, shape or colour, in duplicate or triplicate, depending entirely on the requirements of the business. It is the use and purpose of these documents which is important and which needs to be understood.

Order form

Whenever goods are required an official order form (Fig. 1.2) should be sent to the supplier, giving details of the order, quoting the supplier's catalogue numbers wherever possible and signed by an authorized official. Orders are usually numbered and in duplicate, triplicate or as many copies as are necessary to meet the requirements of the business. The top copy goes to the supplier and the other copies are retained for record or statistical purposes.

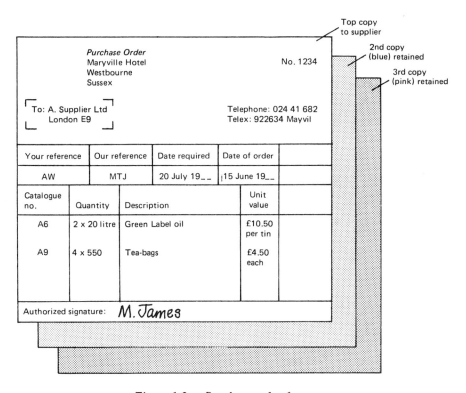

Figure 1.2   *Purchase order form.*

Delivery note

On receipt of an order the supplier will dispatch the goods to the customer with an accompanying delivery note (Fig. 1.3) showing details of goods supplied. The customer should check the goods against the delivery note and before signing for acceptance of the goods any shortages or damages should be noted on all copies. The customer keeps the top copy and the supplier the second copy.

Invoice

An invoice (Fig. 1.4) is a charging document sent by the supplier to the customer. It is numbered and shows details of goods supplied including prices, VAT, packing and delivery charges and details of terms and discounts. Invoices should be checked against the copy order and delivery note. Prices and calculations should be checked and, if correct, the invoice is passed for entry into the book of first entry and from there to the appropriate account in the ledger. (See Chapter 4.)

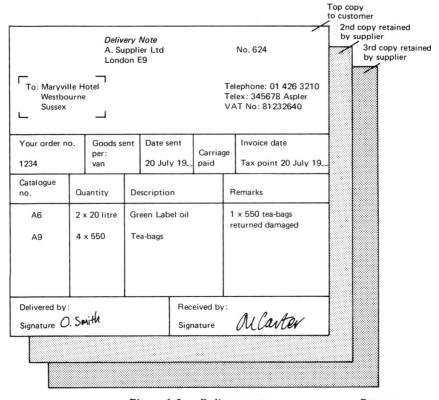

Figure 1.3   *Delivery note.*

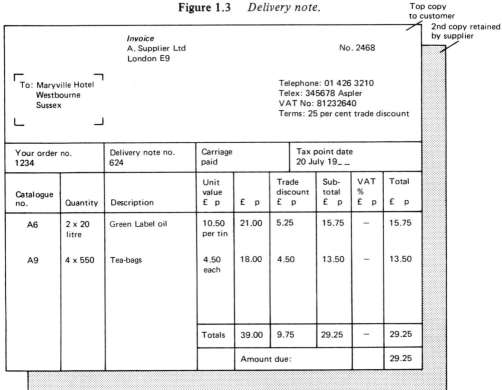

Note: Any chargeable VAT would be added to the amount due.

Figure 1.4   *Invoice.*

Credit note

When goods are returned to the supplier for any reason, for example if they have been damaged in transit or if they are not as ordered, or if there has been an overcharge on an invoice, the supplier will send the customer a credit note (Fig. 1.5) for the amount involved. If correct, the credit note will be passed for entry in the book of first entry and the appropriate ledger account. (See Chapter 4.)

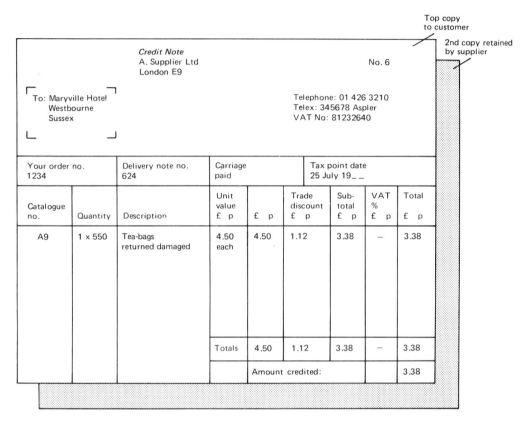

Figure 1.5 *Credit note.*

Debit note

When there has been an undercharge on an invoice the supplier will send the customer a debit note for the amount involved. This acts as a supplementary invoice and, if correct, will be passed and treated in the same manner as an invoice.

Statement

With the mechanization of accounts, invoices and statements are very often written simultaneously, the amounts on the statement being accumulated and the statement (Fig. 1.6) usually being sent by the supplier to the customer at the end of each month. The statement is a summarized account showing the balance that was outstanding at the beginning of the month plus any invoices issued by the supplier during the month, deducting any credit notes, cash paid and discounts allowed. The final figure on the statement is the balance due. The statement is checked against the supplier's account in the ledger and if correct is passed for payment.

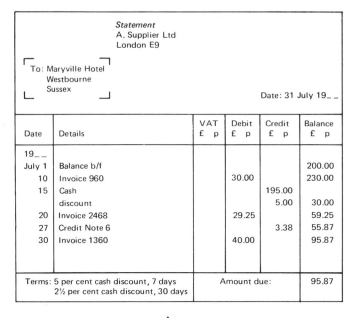

Date	Details	VAT £ p	Debit £ p	Credit £ p	Balance £ p
19__					
July 1	Balance b/f				200.00
10	Invoice 960		30.00		230.00
15	Cash			195.00	
	discount			5.00	30.00
20	Invoice 2468		29.25		59.25
27	Credit Note 6			3.38	55.87
30	Invoice 1360		40.00		95.87

Statement
A. Supplier Ltd
London E9

To: Maryville Hotel
Westbourne
Sussex

Date: 31 July 19__

Terms: 5 per cent cash discount, 7 days
2½ per cent cash discount, 30 days

Amount due: 95.87

Figure 1.6 *Statement.*

ASSIGNMENTS

A1.1   Explain clearly the basic principle and theory of the double-entry book-keeping system.

A1.2   What are the objects and advantages of the double-entry system?

A1.3   Explain the purpose and use of the following business documents, illustrating your answers with diagrams of each document showing all the valid points.

    (a) an order form;
    (b) a delivery note;
    (c) an invoice;
    (d) a credit note;
    (e) a statement.

2 The Ledger

The principal book in the double-entry book-keeping system is the ledger, the term used for a collection of accounts in which all the transactions of the business are recorded either individually or as totals posted from the subsidiary books.

2.1 TYPES OF LEDGER

The traditional ruling of a ledger account is shown below; the page is divided into a left-hand side (debit) and a right-hand side (credit). The act of entering on the left-hand side is called debiting the account and that of entering on the right-hand side is called crediting the account.

Dr. (abbreviation for 'debit') Ledger Account Cr. (abbreviation for 'credit')

Date	Details	F	£	p	Date	Details	F	£	p

The introduction of mechanized accounting has prompted a more up-to-date ruling of the ledger account, as shown below. This type of account is usually in card or loose-leaf form and enables a running balance to be brought out after each transaction has been recorded.

Card or Loose-leaf Ledger Account

Date	Ref.	Details	VAT £ p	Dr. £ p	Cr. £ p	Balance £ p

2.2   CLASSIFICATION OF ACCOUNTS

Accounts in the ledger are divided into two main types:

1. *Personal accounts.* These accounts comprise both debtors and creditors. Debtors are the people who owe money or value to the business, e.g. people to whom the firm has sold goods or given service. Creditors are people to whom the business owes money or value. Personal accounts also include the capital account.
2. *Impersonal accounts.* These again are divided into two classes:
    (a)   Real accounts. These accounts are a record of all the assets of the business, e.g. premises, fixtures and fittings, kitchen equipment, restaurant furniture, china, plate, glassware, office equipment, cash and bank accounts, etc.
    (b)   Nominal accounts. These accounts are a record of the gains, losses and expenses of the business, and include sales, purchases, returns, discounts, and all expense accounts such as wages, heat, light, fuel, advertising, stationery, cleaning materials, rent, rates, insurance, etc.

In practice a separate account is kept in the ledger for each debtor and creditor and for each class of asset, liability or expense incurred by the business.

Example 1: a creditor's account

B. Wright is a supplier to the Royal Hotel, and on 1 January 19__ the hotel owed him £100. On 4 January B. Wright supplied more goods to the hotel valued at £20. On 20 January the hotel paid the amount owing to B. Wright on 1 January less 5 per cent discount. On 21 January B. Wright supplied more goods to the hotel valued at £30. On 31 January the hotel returned goods to B. Wright for which a credit note was received valued at £5. At the end of the month the account was balanced, the balance being brought down to the beginning of next month. B. Wright's account as entered on the traditional-style ledger is shown below, followed by the account as entered on the card or loose-leaf type of ledger in which the balance is brought out after each transaction.

Dr. B. Wright (Creditor) (A/C no. 7) Cr.

Date	Details	F	£	p	Date	Details	F	£	p
19__					19__				
Jan. 20	Cash	CB	95	00	Jan. 1	Balance	b/d	100	00
	Discount		5	00	4	Goods		20	00
31	Returns		5	00	21	Goods		30	00
31	Balance	c/d	45	00					
			150	00				150	00
					Feb. 1	Balance	b/d	45	00

Balancing the account (traditional ledger)

The balance of an account is the difference between the debit side and the credit side. For example, if the credit side of an account adds up to £150 and the debit side adds up to £105 then we would say we have a credit balance of £45.

The procedure for balancing an account is as follows (see above):

1. Add debit side.
2. Add credit side.
3. Take smaller amount from larger amount.
4. Enter the difference on the lighter (or lesser) side with the word 'balance c/d' (carried down).
5. Rule and enter totals of both sides on the same line. They should now add up to the same amount due to the insertion of the balance.
6. Bring down the balance on the heavier (or opposite) side.

B. Wright's account in the card or loose-leaf ledger would be as shown below.

B. Wright (Creditor) (A/C no. 7)

Date	Ref.	Details	Dr.	Cr.	Balance
19__					
Jan. 1		Balance b/f			100.00
4		Goods		20.00	120.00
20		Cash	95.00		
		Discount	5.00		20.00
21		Goods		30.00	50.00
31		Goods returned	5.00		45.00

Note: In a creditor's account all credit entries increase the balance, debit entries decrease the balance, and the figure in the balance column is the amount outstanding at that date.

Example 2: a debtor's account

L. Frost (a debtor) has an account with the Snowdon Hotel. On 1 January she owed £40 to the hotel for luncheons and dinners at the hotel during December. On 17 January she entertained guests at the hotel, bill no. 24, amounting to £35. On 20 January she paid the amount owing on 1 January less 2½ per cent discount. On 27 January her dinner bill no. 123 amounted to £38. On 30 January she was given an allowance of £2 because of an overcharge on a previous bill. The account was balanced as at 31 December. The traditional ledger account and the account as entered on a ledger card are shown below.

Dr.   L. Frost (Debtor) (A/C no. 5)   Cr.

Date	Details	F	£	p	Date	Details	F	£	p
19__					19__				
Jan. 1	Balance	b/d	40	00	Jan. 20	Cash	CB	39	00
17	Bill no. 24		35	00		Discount		1	00
27	Bill no. 123		38	00	30	Allowance		2	00
					31	Balance	c/d	71	00
			113	00				113	00
Feb. 1	Balance	b/d	71	00					

Note: In a debtor's account the balance brought down is on the debit side.

L. Frost (Debtor) (A/C no. 5)

Date	Ref.	Details	Dr.	Cr.	Balance
19__					
Jan. 1		Balance			40.00
17		Bill no. 24	35.00		75.00
20		Cash		39.00	
		Discount		1.00	35.00
27		Bill no. 123	38.00		73.00
30		Allowance		2.00	71.00

Note: In a debtor's account all debit entries increase the balance and credit entries decrease the balance.

Example 3

This example illustrates the posting of an exercise direct to the traditional-style ledger accounts, followed by the same exercise posted to ledger cards. Each follows the rules of the double-entry system in that every debit entry has a corresponding credit entry and vice versa.

19__		Cash or value *in* Account to be debited	Cash or value *out* Account to be credited
Jan. 1	C. Light commenced in business with capital of £25 000 in the bank and £500 cash in hand	Cash/Bank	Capital
2	Purchased restaurant furniture on credit from Fit-Rite Co. Ltd £2000	Restaurant furniture	Fit-Rite Co. Ltd
4	Purchased kitchen equipment on credit from Spooner Ltd £500	Kitchen equipment	Spooner Ltd
15	Bought provisions for cash £150	Purchases	Cash/Bank
25	Sold meals for cash £220	Cash/Bank	Sales
26	Sold meals for cash £120	Cash/Bank	Sales
28	Paid wages by cash £140	Wages	Cash/Bank
30	Paid insurance by cheque £200	Insurance	Cash/Bank
31	Paid rent by cheque £750	Rent	Cash/Bank

This would be posted to the traditional ledger accounts as shown below.

Dr.   Capital (A/C no. 1)   Cr.

Date	Details	F	£	p	Date	Details	F	£	p
					19__				
					Jan. 1	Bank		25 000	00
						Cash		500	00

Dr.   Cash/Bank (A/C no. 2)   Cr.

Date	Details	F	£	p	Date	Details	F	£	p
19_ _					19_ _				
Jan. 1	Capital, C. Light		25 500	00	Jan. 15	Purchases		150	00
25	Sales		220	00	28	Wages		140	00
26	Sales		120	00	30	Insurance		200	00
					31	Rent		750	00
					31	Balance	c/d	24 600	00
			25 840	00				25 840	00
Feb. 1	Balance	b/d	24 600	00					

Dr.   Restaurant Furniture (A/C no. 3)   Cr.

Date	Details	F	£	p	Date	Details	F	£	p
19_ _									
Jan. 2	Fit-Rite Co. Ltd.		2000	00					

Dr.   Fit-Rite Co. Ltd (A/C no. 4)   Cr.

Date	Details	F	£	p	Date	Details	F	£	p
					19_ _				
					Jan. 2	Furniture		2000	00

Dr.   Kitchen Equipment (A/C no. 5)   Cr.

Date	Details	F	£	p	Date	Details	F	£	p
19_ _									
Jan. 4	Spooner Ltd.		500	00					

Dr.   Spooner Ltd (A/C no. 6)   Cr.

Date	Details	F	£	p	Date	Details	F	£	p
					19_ _				
					Jan. 4	Kitchen equipment		500	00

Dr.   Purchases (A/C no. 7)   Cr.

Date	Details	F	£	p	Date	Details	F	£	p
19_ _									
Jan. 15	Cash		150	00					

Dr.   Sales (A/C no. 8)   Cr.

Date	Details	F	£	p	Date	Details	F	£	p
					19_ _				
					Jan. 25	Cash		220	00
					26	Cash		120	00
								340	00

Dr.   Wages (A/C no. 9)   Cr.

Date	Details	F	£	p	Date	Details	F	£	p
19_ _									
Jan. 28	Cash		140	00					

Dr.   Insurance (A/C no. 10)   Cr.

Date	Details	F	£	p	Date	Details	F	£	p
19_ _									
Jan. 30	Cash		200	00					

Dr.   Rent (A/C no. 11)   Cr.

Date	Details	F	£	p	Date	Details	F	£	p
19__ __ Jan. 31	Cash		750	00					

Posting to ledger cards is illustrated below.

Capital (A/C no. 1)

Date	Ref.	Details	Dr.	Cr.	Balance
19__ Jan. 1		Bank		25 000.00	25 000.00
		Cash		500.00	25 500.00 Cr.

Cash/Bank (A/C no. 2)

Date	Ref.	Details	Dr.	Cr.	Balance
19__ Jan. 1		Capital, C. Light	25 500.00		25 500.00
15		Purchases		150.00	25 350.00
25		Sales	220.00		25 570.00
26		Sales	120.00		25 690.00
28		Wages		140.00	25 550.00
30		Insurance		200.00	25 350.00
31		Rent		750.00	24 600.00 Dr.

Restaurant Furniture (A/C no. 3)

Date	Ref.	Details	Dr.	Cr.	Balance
19__ Jan. 2		Fit-Rite Co. Ltd.	2000.00		2000.00 Dr.

Fit-Rite Co. Ltd (A/C no. 4)

Date	Ref.	Details	Dr.	Cr.	Balance
19__ Jan. 2		Restaurant furniture		2000.00	2000.00 Cr.

Kitchen Equipment (A/C no. 5)

Date	Ref.	Details	Dr.	Cr.	Balance
19__ Jan. 4		Spooner Ltd.	500.00		500.00 Dr.

Spooner Co. Ltd (A/C no. 6)

Date	Ref.	Details	Dr.	Cr.	Balance
19__ Jan. 4		Kitchen equipment		500.00	500.00 Cr.

Purchases (A/C no. 7)

Date	Ref.	Details	Dr.	Cr.	Balance
19__ Jan. 15		Cash	150.00		150.00 Dr.

Sales (A/C no. 8)

Date	Ref.	Details	Dr.	Cr.	Balance
19__ Jan. 25		Cash		220.00	220.00
26		Cash		120.00	340.00 Cr.

Wages (A/C no. 9)

Date	Ref.	Details	Dr.	Cr.	Balance
19___ Jan. 28		Cash	140.00		140.00 Dr.

Insurance (A/C no. 10)

Date	Ref.	Details	Dr.	Cr.	Balance
19___ Jan. 30		Cash	200.00		200.00 Dr.

Rent (A/C no. 11)

Date	Ref.	Details	Dr.	Cr.	Balance
19___ Jan. 31		Cash	750.00		750.00 Dr.

2.3 THE TRIAL BALANCE AND SIMPLE FINAL ACCOUNTS

The hotelier and restaurateur sells food, drink and accommodation. In the normal course of business the trader makes a profit by adding a percentage to the cost of goods purchased for resale or to the cost of the service given. The difference between the cost and the selling price is called *gross profit*. From this gross profit must be deducted the expenses of running the business, and the balance left is called the *net profit*. Finally, the trader wishes to know exactly what the business owns (assets) and what it owes (liabilities).

After all transactions are entered in the accounts, to check the accuracy of the double-entry system it will follow that if there has been a debit entry in one account and a credit entry in another account for every transaction, then the total debit balances should equal the total credit balances. This is proved by making a list of all the accounts in the ledger with credit balances and a list of all those with debit balances and, if correct, the two totals should agree. This is known as taking out a trial balance (see Example 4).

When the trial balance has been proved, the trader's final accounts are prepared (see Example 4). These are:

1. The trading account, to find the gross profit.
2. The profit and loss account, to find the net profit.
3. The balance sheet, which is a list of all assets and liabilities.

The step-by-step procedure after the trial balance may be summarized as follows (see Example 4):

1. Transfer purchases to the trading account (debit side).
2. Transfer sales to the trading account (credit side).
3. The difference between purchases and sales is called the gross profit and is transferred to the profit and loss account (credit side).
4. Transfer all expenses to the profit and loss account (debit side).
5. The difference between the gross profit and total expenses is called net profit.
6. The net profit is transferred to the capital account (credit side).
7. All assets with debit balances are transferred to the balance sheet (right-hand side).
8. All liabilities with credit balances are transferred to the balance sheet (left-hand side).

Stock

At the end of the accounting period the stock on hand has to be valued and taken into consideration when preparing the final accounts. Stock is usually valued at the cost price of the goods when purchased or at the current market value, whichever is the lower figure. Stock is a current asset of the business and is shown at the end of the trial balance and in the trading account and balance sheet (see Example 4). Stock at end becomes stock at start when the next trading period commences (see below). The stock account in the ledger would appear as follows:

Dr.							Stock Account			Cr.
Date	Details	F	£	p	Date	Details	F	£	p
19_ _ Jan. 1	Balance from trading account, stock in hand		650	00					

Example 4

The following balances were extracted from the ledger accounts of the Park Hotel and a trial balance, trading account, profit and loss account and balance sheet were prepared.

Park Hotel

Trial Balance as at 31 December 19_ _

Transferred to	Account	Debit balances £	Credit balances £
Balance sheet	Capital		112 960
Balance sheet	Freehold premises	60 000	
Balance sheet	Fixtures and fittings	30 000	
Balance sheet	Kitchen equipment	10 000	
Balance sheet	Restaurant furniture	10 000	
Balance sheet	China, plate and glass	3 000	
Balance sheet	Linen	2 000	
Trading account	Sales		26 145
Trading account	Purchases	10 458	
Balance sheet	Cash	500	
Balance sheet	Bank	3 000	
Balance sheet	Creditors		450
Profit and loss account	Sundry expenses	2 752	
Profit and loss account	Wages	7 845	
		139 555	139 555

Stock at end £650
(Transferred to trading account and balance sheet)

Dr.		Trading Account for year ended 31 December 19_ _		Cr.
	£			£
Purchases	10 458	Sales		26 145
Gross profit c/d	16 337	Stock at end		650
	26 795			26 795

Dr.   Profit and Loss Account for year ended 31 December 19_ _   Cr.

	£		£
Sundry expenses	2 752	Gross profit b/d	16 337
Wages	7 845		
	10 597		
Net profit	5 740		
	16 337		16 337

Dr.   Balance Sheet as at 31 December 19 _ _   Cr.

Liabilities		£	Assets	£
Capital	112 960		Freehold premises	60 000
Add net profit	5 740		Fixtures and fittings	30 000
		118 700	Kitchen equipment	10 000
			Restaurant furniture	10 000
Creditors		450	China, plate and glass	3 000
			Linen	2 000
			Stock at end	650
			Bank	3 000
			Cash	500
		119 150		119 150

ASSIGNMENTS

A2.1 Explain what you understand by a 'debit entry' and a corresponding 'credit entry' in the double-entry book-keeping system.

A2.2 State the account to be debited and the account to be credited for each of the following:

(a) Bought provisions for cash
(b) Paid rent by cheque
(c) Sold meals for cash
(d) Bought kitchen equipment on credit from B. Fine Ltd
(e) Paid insurance by cheque
(f) Bought provisions from B. Grape Ltd
(g) Bought china, plate and glass. Paid by cheque
(h) Paid advertising by cheque
(i) Paid wages by cash
(j) Started business with capital of £50 000 at bank

A2.3 Indicate which of the following accounts are real, which are nominal and which personal:

(a) postage
(b) electricity
(c) purchases
(d) kitchen equipment
(e) sales
(f) advertising
(g) restaurant furniture
(h) cash
(i) L. Frost, a debtor
(j) stationery
(k) office equipment
(l) insurance
(m) B. Wright, a creditor
(n) china, plate and glass
(o) rent
(p) linen
(q) repairs and maintenance
(r) freehold premises
(s) purchases returns
(t) fixtures and fittings

A2.4 L. Sleet is a supplier to the Snowdown Hotel and the following transactions took place during the months of March and April. Illustrate his account as it would appear in the account system of the hotel:

(a) in the traditional-style ledger account;
(b) on a ledger card.

19__
Mar. 1 Balance owing to L. Sleet £120
10 Goods received from L. Sleet value £48
14 Goods received from L. Sleet value £55
20 The hotel paid L. Sleet the amount owing on 1 March less 5 per cent cash discount
22 Credit note for £5 received from L. Sleet in respect of goods returned by the hotel

Mar. 25   Goods received from L. Sleet value £62
           Balance account as at 31 March and continue
Apr. 7   Goods received from L. Sleet value £83
      14   Goods received from L. Sleet value £44
      20   The hotel paid L. Sleet the amount outstanding on 1 April less 5
           per cent cash discount
      24   Credit note for £14 received from L. Sleet in respect of goods
           returned by the hotel
      28   Goods received from L. Sleet value £92
           Balance the account as at 30 April

A2.5   Ms. Flower, a businesswoman, has an account with the Larkspur Hotel. She entertains
business associates at the hotel for lunch or dinner. At the end of each month the
hotel sends Ms. Flower a statement of the amount owing by her to the hotel. The
following transactions took place during the months of January and February. Illustrate Ms. Flower's account with the hotel:

(a) in traditional ledger form;
(b) as it would appear on a ledger card.

Jan. 1   Balance owed to the hotel £40
      3   Luncheons, bill no. 62, £28
      5   Dinners, bill no. 102, £52
      14   Dinners, bill no. 84, £28
      20   Received cheque from Ms. Flower for amount owing on 1 January
           less 2½ per cent discount
      22   Luncheons, bill no. 77, £16
      28   Luncheons, bill no. 88, £26
      28   Allowance of £2 given to Ms. Flower in respect of an overcharge
      30   Dinners, bill no. 144, £52
           Balance the account as at 31 January and continue
Feb. 12   Luncheons, bill no. 22, £15
      18   Luncheons, bill no. 33, £32
      20   Received cheque from Ms. Flower for amount owing on 1 February
           less 2½ per cent discount
      22   Allowance of £3 given in respect of overcharge
      26   Dinners, bill no. 142, £18
      28   Luncheons, bill no. 38, £12
           Balance account as at 28 February

A2.6   (a) Explain the purpose of a trial balance.
        (b) Define the terms 'gross profit' and 'net profit'.
        (c) Define the terms 'assets' and 'liabilities', giving examples in each case.

A2.7 Enter the following transactions in the ledger accounts (either traditional ledger form or on ledger cards) of the Skye Hotel, balance the accounts as at 31 March 19__ and extract a trial balance.

Mar. 1 The business commences with £125 000 capital
2 Paid for leasehold premises £35 000 cheque
4 Paid for kitchen equipment £15 000 cheque
4 Paid for restaurant furniture £7000 cheque
5 Bought china, plate and glassware from Bluett Ltd on credit £1500
5 Bought linen on credit from Warmer Co. £750
6 Bought on credit from Rightway Ltd, fixtures and fittings £2000
15 Bought provisions £300 cheque
15 Bought provisions from Servewell Ltd on credit £500
20 Cash sales £300
21 Cash sales £250
28 Paid wages £150 cash
28 Paid rent £400 cheque

A2.8 Enter the following transactions directly into the ledger accounts (either on ledger cards or in the traditional-style ledger) of the Avery Hotel, balance the accounts as at 31 January and extract a trial balance.

Jan. 1 The business commenced with capital of £125 000 at the bank and £5000 in cash
1 Paid rent by cheque £4000
1 Paid rates by cheque £350
1 Paid insurance by cheque £250
5 Bought kitchen equipment from Spooner and Co. on credit £2000
7 Bought fixtures and fittings from Wessex and Co. Ltd on credit £1500
14 Bought provisions for cash £240
16 Bought provisions for cash £78
18 Bought kitchen equipment from Spooner and Co. on credit £130
21 Paid wages in cash £420
22 Bought provisions for cash £84
23 Cash sales £324
24 Cash sales £280
25 Cash sales £300
27 Paid wages in cash £380
28 Bought fixtures and fittings from Wessex and Co. Ltd on credit £480

A2.9 From the following trial balance prepare the trading account, profit and loss account and balance sheet.

Trial Balance as at 31 December 19_ _

	Dr. £	Cr. £
Capital		286 650
Bank	18 000	
Cash	2 150	
Purchases	41 040	
Sales		108 000
Freehold premises	220 000	
Fixtures and fittings	42 000	
Kitchen equipment	22 000	
Insurance	650	
Rates	1 250	
Sundry expenses	17 540	
Wages	30 240	
Butcher and Co. Ltd		220
	394 870	394 870

Stock at end £500

A2.10 From the following trial balance prepare the trading account, profit and loss account and balance sheet.

Trial Balance as at 31 March 19_ _

	Dr. £	Cr. £
Leasehold premises	70 500	
Fixtures and fittings	40 000	
Kitchen equipment	25 000	
China, glass, cutlery and linen	12 500	
Wages and salaries	38 500	
Heat, light and fuel	6 750	
Repairs and renewals	3 200	
Rent and rates	5 500	
Sundry expenses	3 700	
Creditors		570
Debtors	240	
Cash	630	
Bank	5 750	
Sales		135 000
Purchases	56 700	
Capital		133 400
	268 970	268 970

Stock at end £750

3 The Cash Book

3.1 CASH RECEIPTS AND CASH PAYMENTS

Whether the accounting system of a hotel is mechanized or manual, the basic principles of recording cash receipts and cash payments remain the same. Cash and cheques received will be debited (left-hand side) in the cash book and cash and cheques paid out will be credited (right-hand side) in the cash book. The simplest form of cash book is the three-column ruling shown in Example 1. On the debit side all amounts received in cash are entered in the 'cash' column and amounts that are banked are entered in the 'bank' column. On the credit side all payments made by cash are entered in the 'cash' column and any payments made by cheque are in the 'bank' column.

3.2 DISCOUNTS

Cash discount is a percentage allowance off debts to encourage the customer to pay promptly. If a customer has been allowed a cash discount then the amount is entered in the 'discount allowed' column in the cash receipts book. Any discount that has been received from a supplier is entered in the 'discount received' column in the cash payments book (see Example 1).

3.3 CONTRA ENTRIES IN THE CASH BOOK

In book-keeping a contra entry means a self-balancing entry where there is a debit entry and a corresponding credit entry in the same account. In the cash book, for example, if £400 was taken from the cash till and paid into the bank, then the contra entry would show £400 in the cash column of the cash payments book and £400 in the bank column of the cash receipts book, and a contra sign (¢) would be entered in the folio column on both sides to indicate the transfer (see Example 1). Conversely, if a cheque for £50 were cashed for office use, then the contra entry would show a cheque for £50 entered into the bank column of the cash payments book and the cash coming into the cash column of the cash receipts book (see the three-column cash book).

Three-column Cash Book

Dr.   Cash Receipts

Date	Account to be credited	Folio	Discount allowed	Cash	Bank
19 _ _			£ p	£ p	£ p
Jan. 1	Balance	b/d		130.00	5750.00
2	Cash sales	L.5		250.00	
3	Cash sales	L.5		190.00	
4	Cash	¢			400.00
5	A. Bird	L.6	1.00		39.00
6	Bank	¢		50.00	
7	Cash sales	L.5		220.00	
7	A. Lark (Deposit)	L.7			20.00
			1.00	840.00	6209.00
			L.8		
Jan. 8	Balance	b/d		280.00	5877.00

Cr.   Cash Payments

Date	Account to be debited	Folio	Discount received	Cash	Bank
19 _ _			£ p	£ p	£ p
Jan. 2	Provisions	L.1		40.00	
4	Bank	¢		400.00	
4	Insurance	L.2			130.00
6	J. Wren	L.3	8.00		152.00
6	Wages	L.4		120.00	
6	Cash	¢			50.00
7	Balance	c/d		280.00	5877.00
			8.00	840.00	6209.00
			L.9		

Example 1: three-column cash book

19__		£
Jan. 1	Balance of office cash	130.00
1	Balance at bank	5750.00
2	Cash sales	250.00
2	Bought provisions for cash	40.00
3	Cash sales	190.00
4	Paid cash into bank	400.00
4	Paid insurance by cheque	130.00
5	Received cheque from A. Bird in settlement of his account of £40 less 2½ per cent discount allowed	
6	Paid J. Wren her account of £160 less 5 per cent cash discount	
6	Paid wages in cash	150.00
6	Cashed cheque for office use	50.00
7	Cash sales	220.00
7	Received cheque from A. Lark being deposit paid in advance	20.00

This is shown in the three-column cash book opposite.

3.4 BALANCING THE CASH BOOK

To keep control of the cash on the premises and cash at the bank the cash journals are balanced regularly either weekly or monthly depending on the requirements of the business.

Step-by-step procedures

1. Total discount allowed and discount received columns.
2. Total cash received and cash paid columns.
3. Take cash paid total from cash received total, the difference being the balance, which is entered on the right-hand side, thus making both totals agree (see Example 1).
4. Total bank columns in both cash receipts and cash payments journals.
5. Take bank paid total from bank received column, the difference being the balance, which is added to the right-hand side, thus making both totals agree (see Example 1).
6. Bring cash and bank balances down to the debit side of the cash book (see Example 1).

Posting direct to ledger

Dr. Provisions (A/C no. 1) Cr.

Date	Details	F	£	p	Date	Details	F	£	p
19__ Jan. 2	Cash	CB1	40	00					

Dr. Insurance (A/C no. 2) Cr.

Date	Details	F	£	p	Date	Details	F	£	p
19__ Jan. 4	Cash	CB1	130	00					

Dr.   J. Wren (A/C no. 3)   Cr.

Date	Details	F	£	p	Date	Details	F	£	p
19_ _ Jan. 6	Cash	CB1	152	00	19_ _ Jan. 1	Balance	b/d	160	00
6	Discount	CB1	8	00					

Dr.   Wages (A/C no. 4)   Cr.

Date	Details	F	£	p	Date	Details	F	£	p
19_ _ Jan. 6	Cash	CB1	120	00					

Dr.   Sales (A/C no. 5)   Cr.

Date	Details	F	£	p	Date	Details	F	£	p
					19_ _ Jan. 2	Cash sales	CB1	250	00
					3	Cash sales	CB1	190	00
					7	Cash sales	CB1	220	00

Dr.   A. Bird (A/C no. 6)   Cr.

Date	Details	F	£	p	Date	Details	F	£	p
19_ _ Jan. 1	Balance	b/d	40	00	19_ _ Jan. 5	Cash	CB1	39	00
						Discount	CB1	1	00

Deposits in Advance (A/C no. 7)

Date	Details	F	£	p	Date	Details	F	£	p
					19_ _ Jan. 7	A. Lark	CB1	20	00

Discounts Allowed (A/C no. 8)

Date	Details	F	£	p	Date	Details	F	£	p
19_ _ Jan. 7	Total discounts	CB1	1	00					

Discounts Received (A/C no. 9)

Date	Details	F	£	p	Date	Details	F	£	p
					19_ _ Jan. 7	Total discounts	CB1	8	00

3.5 DEPOSITS IN ADVANCE

When guests are booking accommodation in some hotels it is customary for them to pay a deposit in advance to secure the booking. To record a deposit in advance the cash or cheque received is debited in the cash receipts book (see Example 1), a receipt is sent to the guest, and from the cash receipts book the amount is credited to a composite deposits in advance account in the ledger. When the guest leaves the amount of the deposit is debited in the deposits in advance account and credited to the guest's account on the tabular ledger (see Chapter 6).

3.6 COLUMNAR CASH BOOKS

Many smaller establishments find it useful to use columnar cash books, in which the income and expenditure are analysed under the appropriate headings, as shown below.

Cash Receipts

Date	Account to be credited	Folio	Sales				Total cash	Other receipts	Bank
			Restaurant	Bars	Tobacco	Sundries			

Cash Payments

Date	Account to be debited	Folio	Purchases				Wages	Other payments	Total cash	Bank
			Provisions	Drink	Tobacco	Sundries				

3.7 BANKING

There are many national and international banks and their business is money. The bank provides many services to its customers: it keeps their money safe, and provides a simple means of transferring money from one person to another by use of cheques, bank giro and other methods. The bank also makes available to their customers specialist services for handling tax, investments and so on.

3.8 TYPES OF BANK ACCOUNTS

Providing the bank is satisfied with their letters of reference, people and businesses can open as many accounts with a bank as they wish simply by filling in a form and supplying specimens of the signatures that will be used on cheques. A cheque book and a paying-in book are then supplied and the person or business becomes a holder of an account with that bank. The most common types of account are:

1. Current account. With this type of account money can be paid in, drawn out or transferred to a third party by means of a cheque. No interest is paid on the monies held in the current account.

2. Deposit account. Money that is not required for immediate use can be put into a deposit account which will earn interest calculated on a daily basis. The bank usually likes seven days' notice of withdrawal, otherwise interest will be forfeit.

3.9   TYPES OF CHEQUES

Order cheques

These are uncrossed cheques that can be made payable to a specific person or cash may be given when presented to the bank named on the cheque.

Crossed cheques

This type of cheque is considered safer than an order cheque as cash cannot be paid across the counter for it. Two parallel lines are drawn across the face of the cheque and anyone receiving a crossed cheque must pay it into a bank account. Any specific instructions about how the money has to be transferred can be done by a 'special crossing' being written between the parallel lines (see Fig. 3.1).

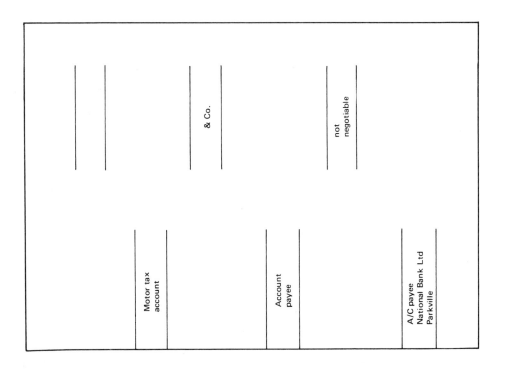

Figure 3.1   *Special crossings.*

Not negotiable

A cheque is a 'negotiable' instrument, which means it can be passed from one person to another, but any person accepting a crossed cheque or a cheque marked 'not negotiable' does so at his or her own risk, subject to any defect in title. This means that if a cheque has been stolen or obtained by fraud then any person accepting or cashing such a cheque may suffer the loss of the value of the cheque.

Example 2

An inexperienced receptionist in a hotel accepts a crossed cheque marked 'not negotiable' from a guest calling himself Mr Robin, without asking for proof of identity. Unknown to the receptionist, Mr Robin was not who he claimed to be and the cheque had been stolen. As Mr Robin did not have legal title to the cheque, he could not pass on the legal title to the hotel. Therefore the bank would not transfer the money and the hotel would suffer the loss.

Example 3

Ms Sparrow, who has no bank account, received a crossed cheque for £20 payable to her. After giving proof of identity she asks a hotelier if he would accept the cheque as payment for her bill of £20. As Ms Sparrow had legal title to the cheque she could pass the cheque on to the hotelier after endorsing it (signing her name) on the back and the bank would honour it. (This is not a practice to be encouraged unless the drawer of the cheque is known by the hotelier to be a person of means.)

3.10   THE CHEQUE BOOK

Cheque books can be issued with either counterfoil (Fig. 3.2) or record slip (Fig. 3.3).

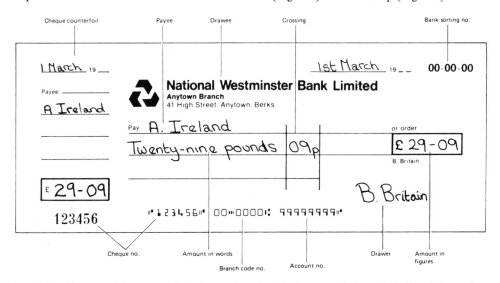

Figure 3.2 *Cheque with counterfoil. Reproduced with the permission of National Westminster Bank Ltd.*

Date	Cheque no.	Cheques issued, credits paid in, other entries	Amount of cheque	Amount of credit	Balance
19__		Balance brought forward			200.00
Jan. 1	601	Electricity Board	38.00		162.00
3	602	B. Smart (provisions)	22.00		140.00
4	—	Cash paid in		520.00	660.00
4	—	Insurance, direct debit	120.00		540.00
5	603	ABC Co. Ltd (wines)	58.00		482.00
Other debits and credits such as standing orders, salary paid direct into bank. Dividends, payments appear on bank statement and should be entered to reconcile with balance.					Balance carried forward

Figure 3.3   *Cheque record slip.*

3.11   ACCEPTING CHEQUES

When accepting a cheque from a guest a receptionist should examine the cheque for the following points:

1. The amount of the cheque should not exceed the limit set by the management. If it does the management's instructions on how to deal with it should be followed.
2. The date of the cheque must not be a future one, nor must it be out of date (more than six months old).
3. The hotel must be named as the payee.
4. The words and figures should agree, and if either have been altered the drawer must sign the alteration.
5. The cheque must be signed by the drawer.
6. The guest should sign his or her name on the back and proof of identity should be given. If, however, a cheque guarantee card is being used it is only necessary to write the card number on the back of the cheque once the expiry date, code number and signature have been verified.

3.12   DISHONOURED CHEQUES

A bank will dishonour a cheque and return it to the payee for any of the following reasons:

1. If there are insufficient funds in the drawer's account. (The cheque is normally marked R/D, which means 'refer to drawer'.)
2. If there is no signature on the cheque.
3. If the signature is incorrect.
4. If the words and figures do not agree.
5. If the cheque is stale (more than six months old) or postdated (future date).
6. If the cheque is badly mutilated.
7. If the drawer dies suddenly.

3.13 BANK GIRO CREDIT SLIPS

This is a system by which one cheque is issued to pay several bills simultaneously. A trader may give his or her bank a list of creditors to be paid, along with the names of their banks; the bank then transfers to the creditors' banks the appropriate amounts and deducts the total sum from the trader's account. (See Fig. 3.4.)

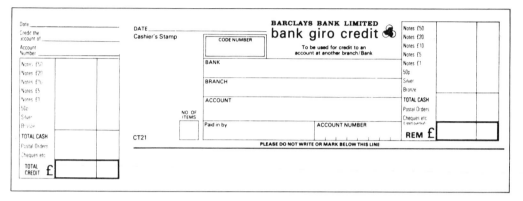

Figure 3.4 *Bank giro credit. Reproduced with the permission of Barclays Bank Ltd.*

3.14 CHEQUE CARDS

A cheque card (Fig. 3.5) is issued at the bank's discretion and enables the drawer to draw up to £50 at any branch of most banks. It also makes most cheques up to £50 acceptable in hotels, shops and garages by guaranteeing the amount of the cheque.

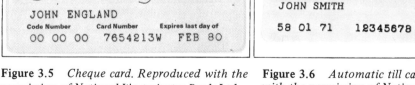

Figure 3.5 *Cheque card. Reproduced with the permission of National Westminster Bank Ltd.*

Figure 3.6 *Automatic till card. Reproduced with the permission of National Westminster Bank Ltd.*

3.15 STANDING ORDERS

A customer may instruct his or her bank to make regular payments on his or her behalf, e.g.

rent, rates, insurance, mortgage repayments, hire-purchase repayments, etc., by completing a standing order form at the bank. The bank will continue to make these payments until the standing order is cancelled.

3.16   LOANS AND OVERDRAFTS

A loan is money borrowed over a certain period of time. It is a liability of a business, and the interest charged on the loan is an expense to the business. An overdraft is when the customer has permission to overdraw his or her account at the bank by a set sum on which the bank will charge interest. If a business has an overdraft the bank balance would be on the credit side of the cash book.

3.17   AUTOMATIC TILL CARD

This card (Fig. 3.6) gives 24-hour access to cash, within a limit previously agreed with the bank, by means of an automatic till outside the bank. By placing the card in the appropriate slot and tapping the correct digits money can be obtained, cheque books or statements can be ordered, and during a working day a balance of the customer's account can be obtained.

3.18   ACCESS, BARCLAYCARD, EUROCARD

Banks will issue these credit cards (Fig. 3.7) free to their customers. The customer can use the card to buy goods or services by signing a sales voucher for the total amount of the bill, and the credit card company then sends a monthly statement to the customer detailing the purchases and the amount owing. If the customer pays within a certain time limit the amount is interest free, but after that time interest in charged for the amount outstanding. The banks issue the credit card only after they are satisfied of the credit-worthiness of the customer. These credit cards are accepted by most hotels as a method of payment.

Figure 3.7   *Access and Barclaycard. Reproduced with permission.*

Figure 3.8 *Diners Club International, Carte Blanche and American Express. Reproduced with permission.*

3.19 OTHER CREDIT CARDS

There are other credit card companies whose cards are accepted worldwide and who allow the customer unlimited credit. These companies charge an annual subscription and the customer has to settle each month's statement in full. Examples are American Express, Diners Club International and Carte Blanche. (See Fig. 3.8.)

3.20 EUROCHEQUE

A Eurocheque requires special international clearance, so it is customary to make an additional charge to the amount that is being settled by Eurocheque, e.g. a bill for £70 plus 70p for special clearance. When being paid in to the bank Eurocheques are listed on a separate paying-in slip.

3.21 CLEARING A CHEQUE

It is customary to allow at least three to four days for a cheque to be cleared and the money transferred from one account to another.

Figure 3.9   *Eurocard symbol.*

3.22   EUROCARD SYMBOL

This (Fig. 3.9) allows a customer to cash cheques, up to the limit specified on the card, in foreign countries. The cheque can be converted into foreign currency at the prevailing exchange rate.

3.23   ACCEPTING PAYMENT BY CREDIT CARD

1. Check that the total amount of the bill is within the 'floor limit'. This is the maximum amount that can be accepted by a hotel or restaurant on a credit card without telephoning for authorization.
2. Write out a sales voucher and ask the customer for the credit card.
3. Make an imprint of the credit card onto the sales voucher.
4. Retain the card and pass the sales voucher to guest to be signed.
5. Check the signature against the signature on the credit card.
6. Return the credit card to the guest with one copy of the sales voucher.

3.24   ACCOUNTING FOR PAYMENT BY CREDIT CARD

As most establishments now accept payment by credit card the procedure for obtaining payment is as follows:

1. Bank credit card sales vouchers can be debited in the cash book along with other cash or cheques which have to be paid into the bank. It is customary for the credit card companies to deduct their commission from the total sum of the sales voucher and pay the balance, so the cash book must show the difference as commission allowed and post it to the ledger account for commissions as an expense.
2. The sales vouchers for other types of credit cards, e.g. Diners Club International or American Express, are sent to the credit card company every few weeks and a cheque is returned in payment less any commission allowed. The cheque received and commission allowed are debited in the cash book and credited to the appropriate accounts in the ledger.

3.25 TRAVELLER'S CHEQUES

These (Fig. 3.10) can be obtained from any bank or travel agency, and are usually issued in either the currency of the home country of the traveller or in the currency of the country he or she is visiting. When receiving the cheques from the bank or travel agency the traveller has to sign them in front of the cashier, and when they are being cashed or used for payment they must be signed again and anyone accepting them must check that the signatures correspond. If there is any doubt one should tactfully ask for proof of identity. Lists of stolen or lost traveller's cheques are sometimes circulated to hotels and these should be consulted.

3.26 TRAVEL AGENTS' VOUCHERS

Some travel agents issue their clients with vouchers which can be used to settle their hotel bills. One copy of the voucher is usually sent to the hotel with the booking and the other is presented by the guest on arrival. All vouchers are sent back to the individual agents, usually at the end of the month. When the agents pay the amount due on the vouchers they will subtract their agreed commission. The cheques and commissions are debited in the cash book and posted to the appropriate accounts in the ledger.

Figure 3.10 *Traveller's cheque. Reproduced with the permission of National Westminster Bank Ltd.*

3.27   FOREIGN CURRENCY

Most large hotels which cater for foreign visitors offer foreign exchange facilities to their guests; in other words they will change foreign currency for the currency of the home country or accept foreign currency in payment for their bill. The exchange rate offered by hotels is usually lower than the bank exchange rate so that the hotel will make a profit on each transaction. Exchange rate tables are usually displayed in the reception office, as rates can fluctuate daily.

Exchange Rate Table (Complete this table with the present-day rates.)

Jamesville Hotel   Exchange Rate on 15 August 19_ _ £1.00 =

Australia	– Dollar	Italy – Lira	Turkey – Lira
Austria	– Schilling	Japan – Yen	USA – Dollar
Belgium	– Franc	Malta – Pound	Yugoslavia – Dinar
Canada	– Dollar	Morocco – Dirham	
Denmark	– Krone	New Zealand – Dollar	
Eire	– Pound	Norway – Krone	
Finland	– Marka	Portugal – Escudo	
W. Germany	– Deutschmark	Spain – Peseta	
Greece	– Drachma	Sweden – Krona	
Holland	– Guilder	Switzerland – Franc	
		Saudi Arabia – Riyal	
		Tunisia – Dinar	
		South Africa – Rand	

3.28   PAYING IN

Paying-in books are issued by the bank. They are stamped with the name, number and details of the owner's account (see Fig. 3.11). The hotel cashier should separate the notes into their separate denominations and stack them face upwards in the same direction; coins should be stacked for easy counting. Foreign currency should be separated into their various countries and denominations, and cheques, traveller's cheques and credit card sales vouchers should all be stacked in their appropriate piles. The paying-in slips are then completed (separate ones for credit vouchers and foreign currency) and the totals checked against the various stacks before being bundled into the appropriate bags supplied by the bank. The total amounts of cash, cheques, etc. are then entered into the cash receipts book from the paying-in slip. When the money is handed in to the bank, the bank cashier will check it and stamp the counterfoil if it is correct. The bank retains the top copy and the second copy remains in the paying-in book for record purposes. The bank will later let the customer know the sterling value given for foreign currency.

3.29   BANK RECONCILIATION STATEMENTS

Usually at the end of the month the bank will send its customers a statement of their account which will show details of amounts paid in, cheques drawn out, standing orders, bank giro credits,

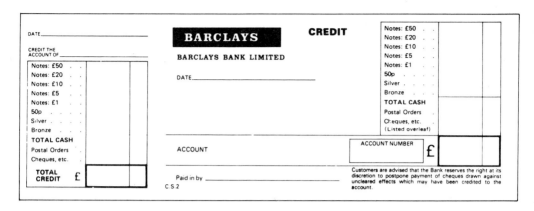

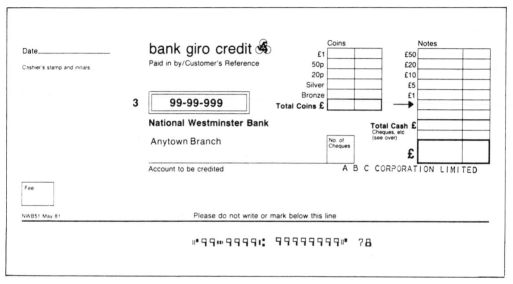

Figure 3.11 *Paying-in slips. Reproduced with permission.*

etc., and the final balance at the bank. As the customer is a creditor of the bank a credit balance (Cr.) means there is money in the account, while a debit balance (Dr.) indicates that the account is overdrawn. In theory the entries on the bank statement should correspond with entries in the cash receipts and cash payments books. However, in practice, the balance of the bank statement and the balance as shown by the cash book rarely agree. A bank reconciliation is therefore prepared to show how this difference has arisen and to bring the balance of the bank statement and the balance in the cash book into agreement. This difference may be caused by the following (see cash book and bank statement below):

1. Cheques debited in the cash receipts book but not yet credited by the bank.
2. Cheques credited in the cash payments book but not yet presented for payment to the bank.
3. Items shown on the bank statement but not yet entered into the cash book, such as standing orders, direct debits, bank giro credits, interest charges on overdrafts, dividends paid direct to the bank, bank charges, etc.

Cash Receipts			Cash Payments			
Date	Details	Bank	Date	Details	Cheque no.	Bank
19__		£	19__			£
Mar. 1	Balance	1500.00	Mar. 5	L. Reddy and Co.	001	75.00
3	Cash sales banked	700.00	7	Wages	002	350.00
7	A. Gem Ltd	50.00	11	B. Bluett	003	120.00
7	Cash sales banked	600.00	14	Wages	004	380.00
14	O. Perl and Co.	175.00	15	Fit-Rite Ltd	005	250.00
21	Cash sales banked	750.00	21	Wages	006	320.00
27	Cash sales banked	720.00	24	C. Green and Co.	007	170.00
31	K. Ruby	36.00	28	Wages	008	360.00
31	Cash sales banked	740.00				

Note: Only the bank column of the cash book is illustrated.

Bank Statement

Date	Details	Debit	Credit	Balance
19__		£	£	£
Mar. 1	Balance			1500.00
3	Cash/cheques		700.00	2200.00
7	Cash/cheques		50.00	2250.00
7	Cash/cheques		600.00	2850.00
7	002	350.00		2500.00
9	001	75.00		2425.00
14	003	120.00		2305.00
14	Cash/cheques		175.00	2480.00
14	004	380.00		2100.00
21	Cash/cheques		750.00	2850.00
21	005	250.00		2600.00
21	006	320.00		2280.00
27	Cash/cheques		720.00	3000.00
28	008	360.00		2640.00
31	Bank giro credit		30.00	2670.00
31	Standing order 126	140.00		2530.00

Step-by-step procedure

If the cash book has not been balanced:

1. Tick off all items that appear both in cash book and in the bank statement and put a cross by items which do not appear in both.
2. Enter in the cash book items that appear only in the bank statement, e.g. bank giro credits, standing orders, etc.
3. Balance the cash book and prepare a bank reconciliation statement as follows:

Bank Reconciliation Statement as at 31 March 19__

	£	£
Balance as per bank statement		(Cr.) 2530.00
Add cheques not yet credited		
K. Ruby	36.00	
Cash sales	740.00	776.00
		3306.00
Less cheques not yet presented		
007	170.00	170.00
Balance as per cash book		(Dr.) 3136.00

Note: Check this against the cash book balance after entering in the cash book items that appear only in the bank statement.

If the cash book has been balanced:

1. Tick off all items which appear both in the cash book and in the bank statement and put a cross by those items which do not appear in both.
2. Any item which has been credited on the bank statement would be deducted in the bank reconciliation statement, e.g. bank giro credit £30.
3. Any item which has been debited in the bank statement would be added in the bank reconciliation statement, e.g. standing order £140.
4. Prepare the bank reconciliation statement as follows:

Bank Reconciliation Statement as at 31 March 19__

	£		£
Balance as per bank statement		(Cr.)	2530.00
Add cheques not yet credited			
K. Ruby	36.00		
Cash sales	740.00		
Standing order	140.00		916.00
			3446.00
Less cheques not yet presented			
007	170.00		
Bank giro credit	30.00		200.00
Balance as per cash book		(Dr.)	3246.00

Note: Balance the cash book and check it against the bank reconciliation balance.

If the bank reconciliation statement commences with the cash book balance the procedure is reversed:

Bank Reconciliation Statement as at 31 March 19__

	£		£
Balance as per cash book		(Dr.)	3246.00
Add cheques not yet presented			
007	170.00		
Bank giro credit	30.00		200.00
			3446.00
Less cheques not yet credited			
K. Ruby	36.00		
Cash sales	740.00		
Standing order	140.00		916.00
Balance as per bank statement		(Cr.)	2530.00

An account with an overdraft (debit balance with the bank)

When there is an overdraft at the bank the procedure would be reversed:

1. Cheques not yet presented would increase the overdraft and so would be added to the bank statement balance.
2. Cheques not yet credited would reduce the overdraft and so would be deducted from the bank statement balance.
3. Any items appearing on the bank statement but not entered in the cash book which have increased the overdraft would be deducted in the bank reconciliation statement, e.g. interest on overdraft.

4. Any items appearing on the bank statement but not entered in the cash book which have decreased the overdraft would be added in the bank reconciliation statement, e.g. bank giro credit.
5. Prepare the bank reconciliation statement as follows:

	£
Balance as per bank statement 31 March 19__ (Dr.)	420.00
Cheques not yet credited	120.00
Cheques not yet presented	60.00
Bank giro credit	42.00
Interest on overdraft	5.00

Bank Reconciliation Statement as at 31 March 19__

	£		£
Balance as per bank statement		(Dr.)	420.00
Add cheques not yet presented	60.00		
Bank giro credit	42.00		102.00
			522.00
Less cheques not yet credited	120.00		
Interest on overdraft	5.00		125.00
Balance as per cash book		(Cr.)	397.00

If the bank reconciliation statement commences with the cash book balance the procedure is reversed:

Bank Reconciliation Statement as at 31 March 19__

	£		£
Balance as per cash book		(Cr.)	397.00
Add cheques not yet credited	120.00		
Interest on overdraft	5.00		125.00
			522.00
Less cheques not yet presented	60.00		102.00
Bank giro credit	42.00	(Dr.)	420.00
Balance as per bank statement			

3.30　CASH FLOATS

Cash floats are the fixed sums of cash that are handed out to the various departments such as restaurants and bars so that they have cash available for change to start the day's business. The number and size of cash floats will depend on the requirements of the sales outlets in the hotel. They must be controlled, checked and accounted for at the end of each session of business. The chief cashier will have a record of the amount of cash which is allocated to each float and will take this into consideration when reconciling the cash in the cash book.

3.31　THE PETTY CASH BOOK

Petty cash must not be confused with cash floats. Most businesses keep a petty cash book to record all small items of expenditure. The safest method of keeping petty cash is on the imprest system, by which the petty cashier is entrusted with a fixed sum of money out of which all small payments are made. An analysed petty cash book is ruled up and a voucher is signed whenever cash is paid out. Periodically, when the imprest is getting low, the petty cashier presents the petty cash book, receipts and vouchers to the head cashier, who will audit them (check them). If all is correct the petty cashier will receive a reimbursing amount of cash or a cheque which can be cashed for the total spent which will bring the petty cash float up to the original imprest. The chief cashier posts the amount of the cash or cheque to the cash payments book.

Advantages of the imprest system

1. The amount that can be stolen is limited to the amount of the imprest.
2. All small items of expenditure are kept out of the main cash book, thus saving time and space.
3. Small items of expenditure can be analysed and controlled, which is important, as these can add up considerably over a period of time.
4. There is a regular audit on petty cash expenditure, thus controlling fraud.
5. The petty cashier has to account for the imprest in his or her charge.

VPOs (visitors' paid-outs)

VPOs, sometimes referred to as disbursements, are any items of cash paid out on behalf of the guests in the hotel, e.g. for taxis, flowers, magazines. These items are entered in the petty cash book in the special VPOs column and posted to the guests' accounts on the tabular ledger (see Chapter 6).

Example

On 1 January 19__ the petty cashier received an imprest of £40 and paid out the following items of expenditure:

    Jan. 2 Bought postage stamps £7.50
         3 Paid for flowers, Mrs Young, Room 21, £1.50
         3 Paid for taxi fare for director £4.00
         4 Bought biros and sticky tape £1.85
         4 Bought trade magazines £0.90
         5 Paid chef's fares £0.80
         5 Paid for taxi, Mr Older, Room 18, £2.50
         6 Bought carbon paper for office £3.75
         6 Paid for advertisement £4.00
         7 Paid for specially printed menus £5.00
         7 Paid for advertisement £2.00
         8 Paid postage on parcel £1.45
         8 Paid postage on parcel for Miss Youth, Room 201, £1.60
         8 Balanced petty cash book (see below) and obtained a reimbursing cheque
            (cash).

(The balance should correspond with the amount of petty cash the cashier has in hand. The reimbursing cheque should correspond with the amount spent.)

Petty Cash Book

Cash received	Date	Details	Voucher no.	Total	Postage and telegrams	Printing and stationery	Advertising	Travelling expenses	Sundry expenses	VPOs
£	19__			£	£	£	£	£	£	£
40.00	Jan. 1	Imprest	—	—						
	2	Postage stamps	1	7.50	7.50					
	3	Flowers, Mrs Young, Room 21	2	1.50						1.50
	3	Taxi, director	3	4.00				4.00		
	4	Biros, sticky tape	4	1.85		1.85				
	4	Trade magazines	5	0.90					0.90	
	5	Chef's fares	6	0.80				0.80		
	5	Taxi, Mr Older, Room 18	7	2.50						2.50
	6	Carbon paper	8	3.75		3.75				
	6	Advertisement	9	4.00			4.00			
	7	Printed menus	10	5.00		5.00				
	7	Advertisement	11	2.00			2.00			
	8	Postage on parcel	12	1.45	1.45					
	8	Postage on parcel, Miss Youth, Room 201	13	1.60						1.60
				36.85	8.95	10.60	6.00	4.80	0.90	5.60
	8	Balance	c/d	3.15	L.3	L.4	L.5	L.6	L.7	
40.00				40.00		All totals debited to their respective expense accounts in ledger				Each item debited individually to guest's account on tabular ledger
3.15	8	Balance	b/d	—						
36.85	8	Reimbursing cheque	—	—						

ASSIGNMENTS

A3.1 (a) Explain the difference between a current and a deposit account.
  (b) Explain the difference between an order and a crossed cheque.
  (c) Give three examples of a special crossing.
  (d) Draw a specimen crossed cheque with counterfoil and name:
    (i) the drawer;
    (ii) the drawee;
    (iii) the payee.
  (e) Explain the terms:
    (i) 'endorsing' a cheque;
    (ii) 'not negotiable';
    (iii) a cheque marked 'RD'.
  (f) List the points a receptionist must note when accepting a cheque from a guest in payment of his or her bill.
  (g) Explain briefly the purpose and nature of the following:
    (i) cheque cards;
    (ii) bank giro slips;
    (iii) standing orders;
    (iv) service cards;
    (v) Access, Barclaycard, Eurocheque and other credit cards;
    (vi) Traveller's cheques;
    (vii) Travel agents' vouchers.
  (h) Explain clearly the step-by-step procedure for accepting payment by credit card.
  (i) Explain briefly the method of accounting for payment by credit card.
  (j) (i) Explain the correct method of handling cash, cheques, etc., in preparation for completing the paying-in slip and banking.
    (ii) Draw up a specimen paying-in slip and enter the following:

2 × £50 notes	21 × 50p pieces
6 × £10 notes	77 × 10p pieces
25 × £5 notes	15 × 5p pieces
72 × £1 notes	35 × 2p pieces
	12 × 1p pieces

3 Personal cheques, £15, £17.50, £44

A3.2 Record the following transactions in the three-column cash book of the Essex Hotel and balance as at 31 March 19__.

Mar. 27 Balance at bank £820
  Balance in cash £55
  28 Received cheque from W. Holmes being settlement of his account of £480 after taking 12½ per cent discount
  28 Cash sales £133
  28 Paid L. Mason a cheque for £275 in settlement of her account for £300
  29 Cash sales £220
  29 Paid wages cash £100
  29 Paid advertising £20 cash
  30 Paid £150 cash into bank

Mar. 30 Bought provisions £33 cheque
30 Paid rent £80 cheque

A3.3 Record the following transactions in the three-column cash book of the York Hotel.

Jan. 1 Balance b/d £50 in cash and £1000 in bank
2 Bought purchases £115 cheque
3 Cash sales £35
4 Paid rent £25 cheque
4 Cash purchases £40
4 Cash sales £85
5 Paid wages £15 cash
5 Paid £110 cash into bank
7 Cash sales £35
7 Paid rates £27 cash
8 Cashed cheque for office use £25
10 Cash sales £55
10 Paid wages £15 cash
11 Paid £75 cash into bank
11 Received cheque from S. White £120 in full settlement of his account of £125
12 Paid cheque in full settlement of B. Brown's account of £250 less 5 per cent discount
Balance cash book and bring down balance

A3.4 Record the following transactions in the three-column cash book of the Sussex Hotel.

Jan. 1 Balance b/d £4500 at bank and £500 cash in hand
2 Cash sales £250
2 Paid rent by cheque £750
2 Paid for provisions by cash £150
3 Received cheque from T. Jones in full settlement of his account of £400 less 5 per cent discount
3 Cash sales £225
4 Paid wages £85 cash
4 Paid £150 cash into bank
4 Paid cheque to V. Snow in settlement of her account of £80 less 2½ per cent discount
5 Cash sales £175
5 Paid insurance by cheque £130
5 Paid wages £33 cash
6 Paid sundry expenses cash £15
7 Paid £300 cash into bank
Balance cash book as at 7 January

A3.5 Record the following transactions in the three-column cash book of the Devon Hotel and balance as at 7 January 19_ _

Jan. 1 Balance b/d £240 in cash and £4300 at bank

Jan. 2   Cash sales £480.75

2   Received cash from L. Toms £85.50 after allowing a £4.50 discount

3   Paid £600 cash into bank

4   Paid for purchases £230 cheque

4   Paid rent £100 cheque

4   Cashed cheque for office use £80

4   Received cheque from S. Green in settlement of his account of £500 less 12½ per cent cash discount

5   Paid wages £50 cash

5   S. Green's cheque was returned by bank marked RD

5   Proprietor withdrew £20 cash for personal use

6   Banked cash sales £500.80

A3.6   Record the following transactions in the three-column cash book of the Berks Hotel.

Jan. 1   Balance at bank £1500

         Balance in cash £80

1   Cash sales £230

2   Insurance by cheque £178

4   Cash sales £290

4   Paid cheque to E. Seabright in settlement of her account of £180 less 5 per cent cash discount

5   Cash sales £320

5   Paid cash into bank £800

6   Paid wages in cash £100

7   Cashed cheque for office use £50

7   Cash sales £340

7   Received cheque from Pebble and Co. in settlement of their account of £220 less 2½ per cent cash discount

7   Paid for provisions by cash £20

7   Balance cash book, bring down balances and continue

Jan. 8   Cash sales £350

8   Paid electricity by cheque £78

8   Paid for provisions by cash £60

9   Cash sales £320

9   Banked all cash except £20

10   Paid rates by cheque £120

10   Cash sales £290

12   Pebble and Co.'s cheque returned marked RD

12   Paid wages by cash £140

12   Proprietor withdrew cash £100

12   Paid for provisions by cash £35

13   Cashed cheque for office use £50

14   Received cheque from Beach Ltd in settlement of their account of £160 less 2½ per cent cash discount

14   Cash sales £420

14   Banked all cash except £25

         Balance the cash book and bring down the balances as at 14 January

A3.7   Rule up a petty cash book with analysis columns for postage and telegrams, printing and stationery, travelling expenses, sundry expenses and VPOs and enter the
following:

19__

Mar.	1	Received cheque imprest £15
	1	Paid travelling expenses £1.75
	2	Bought postage stamps £3
	2	Paid for flowers £1.60
	3	Paid taxi fare for Mr Jones, Room 126, £1.35
	3	Paid tip to delivery woman 20p
	4	Bought envelopes 55p
	4	Paid postage 85p
	4	Paid bus fares 22p
	5	Paid newspapers for Mr Smith, Room 23, 45p
	5	Bought carbon paper £1.40
		Balance petty cash book and obtain reimbursing cheque from chief cashier

A3.8   Rule up a petty cash book with suitable columns and record the following transactions.

19__

Jan.	1	Balance in hand £30.50
	1	Received reimbursing cheque from chief cashier to make up imprest to £40
	2	Paid for postage stamps £3
	3	Paid postage for Ms Jones, Room 67, £1.04
	4	Paid for carbon paper £1.88
	5	Paid for shorthand notebook £1
	6	Paid for parcel, Mr Brown, Room 36, 40p
	7	Paid bus fare for porter 50p
	8	Paid carriage on small parcel 90p
	9	Paid for gift box, Ms Barry, Room 15, £2.10
	10	Paid for string and labels £1.52
	11	Paid taxi for manager £4
	12	Paid window cleaner £7
	13	Paid railway fares for porter £3.06
	14	Paid advertisement 80p
	15	Paid for magazine, Mr Allan, Room 63, 90p
	16	Paid postage £4 and advertising £2.20
	17	Balance and obtain reimbursing cheque from head cashier

A3.9   Explain what is meant by the imprest system of keeping petty cash.

A3.10   Rule up a petty cash book with suitable columns and record the following petty cash
disbursements, balancing and obtaining a reimbursing cheque when necessary.

19__

Jan.	1	Balance in hand £15.25

Jan. 1   Received reimbursing cheque to bring imprest up to £30
    2   Paid for postage stamps £5
    3   Paid for postage for Ms Jones, Room 201, £1.25
    4   Paid for trade magazines 50p
    5   Paid for shorthand notebooks £3.50
    5   Paid for printing special menus £3
    6   Paid postage on parcel for Mrs Brown, Room 206, 60p
    7   Paid taxi fare for porter £1.20
    7   Paid excess postage on letter 25p
    8   Paid for gift box for Mr Barry, Room 107, 45p
    9   Paid for string, labels, sticky tape £2.30
   10   Paid donation to charity 50p
   11   Paid florist £3.50
   12   Paid taxi for porter £1.50
   13   Paid for advertisement £4
   14   Paid for magazines for Ms Allen, Room 204, £1.25
   16   Paid for postage stamps £5
   17   Paid for flowers, Mrs Brown, Room 206, £1.30
   17   Paid for taxi, Ms Jones, Room 201, £3
   18   Paid taxi for director £2.50
   18   Paid florist £4.50
   18   Paid for magazines £1.75
   19   Paid taxi for Ms Jones, Room 201, £2
   20   Paid advertisement £4
   22   Paid for carbon paper £3.75
   22   Balance and obtain reimbursing cheque from chief cashier

A3.11   Explain the purpose of preparing a bank reconciliation statement.

A3.12   From the following cash book and bank statement prepare a bank reconciliation statement as at 31 March 19___.

	Cash Receipts					Cash Payments			
Date	Details	F	£ p		Date	Details	Cheque no.	F	£ p
19__					19__				
Mar. 24	Balance	b/d	1049.71		Mar. 26	A. Rose Ltd	577		80.50
27	Sales		596.75		26	Eastern Gas	578		61.79
28	Sales		579.00		26	B. Lily and Co.	579		50.00
29	Stalk and Co.		250.00		26	C. Thorne Ltd	580		189.25
30	Sales		620.00		27	Wages	581		450.00
31	Budd Ltd		92.00		28	Petal Ltd	582		92.16
31	Sales		510.00		28	Electricity	583		114.00
					30	W. Stem Ltd	584		24.20

Bank Statement

Date	Details	Dr.	Cr.	Balance
19__		£	£	£
Mar. 24	Balance			1049.71
27	Cash/Cheques		596.75	1646.46
28	Cash/Cheques		579.00	2225.46
29	577	80.50		2144.96
29	Cash/Cheques		250.00	2394.96
30	578	61.79		2333.17
30	580	189.25		2143.92
30	Cash/Cheques		620.00	2763.92
31	581	450.00		2313.92
31	Bank giro credit		200.00	2513.92
31	Standing order (insurance)	160.00		2353.92
31	Bank charges	16.42		2337.50

A3.13 Prepare a bank reconciliation statement from the following information:

		£
Cash book balance 30 June 19__	(Dr.)	530.00
Balance as per bank statement	(Cr.)	471.00
Unpresented cheques		170.00
Cheques not yet credited		330.00
Dividend on investments not entered in cash book		120.00
Standing order not entered in cash book		19.00

A3.14 Prepare a bank reconciliation statement from the following information:

		£
Cash book balance 31 January 19__	(Dr.)	269.40
Balance as per bank statement 31 January 19__	(Dr.)	600.00
Unpresented cheques		320.60
Cheques not yet credited by bank		1200.00
Interest on overdraft not entered in cash book		15.00
Bank giro credit not entered in cash book		25.00

A3.15 Convert the following foreign currencies into sterling using the current rates of exchange.

(a) 3200 French francs;
(b) 24 000 Italian lire;
(c) 750 American dollars;
(d) 378 Deutschmarks;
(e) 825 Spanish pesetas;
(f) 230 Dutch guilders;
(g) 450 Norwegian kroner;
(h) 660 Portuguese escudos;
(i) 825 Greek drachmas;
(j) 2500 Japanese yen.

4 Purchases, Sales and Returns

In business the term 'purchases' means those goods that are bought from a supplier for resale at a profit. In the hotel and catering industry it is usually food, drink and tobacco that are purchased for resale.

4.1 CASH PURCHASES

When food, drink or tobacco is purchased and the payment is made by cash at the time of the purchase, then to record this type of transaction is simple:

1. The cash payments book is credited with the cash paid out for the goods (see Example 1).
2. The purchases account is debited with the amount paid for goods coming in (see Example 1).

Example 1

19_ _
Jan. 1 The Clyde Hotel bought provisions valued at £40, payment being made by cash

Dr.	Cash Receipts						Cash Payments			Cr.
Date	Details	F	Cash	Bank	Date	Details	F	Cash	Bank	
					19_ _			£		
					Jan. 1	Provisions	L5	40.00		

Dr.				Purchases (A/C no. 5)					Cr.	
Date	Details	F	£	p	Date	Details	F	£	p	
19_ _										
Jan. 1	Cash	CB	40	00						

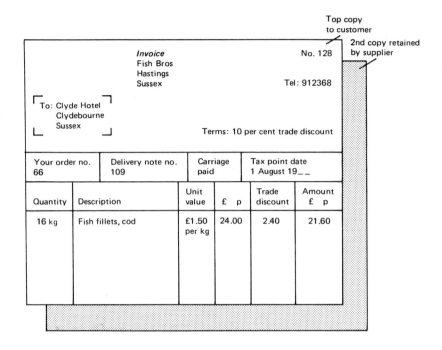

Figure 4.1   *An invoice from a supplier.*

4.2   CREDIT PURCHASES

It is common business practice for suppliers to send goods to their customers and for the customers to pay at a later date, usually the month following delivery. Goods purchased by this method are classified as credit purchases and are dealt with in the accounts system as follows:

1. The goods are ordered.
2. The supplier sends the goods accompanied by a delivery note.
3. An invoice (Fig. 4.1) is received detailing the prices and value of goods supplied.
4. The invoice is checked and, if correct, is entered into the purchases daybook (shown below).
5. The amount of the invoice is then posted from the purchases daybook to the supplier's account in the ledger on the credit (right-hand) side, as the supplier has now become a creditor of the business.
6. The monthly total of credit purchases is posted from the purchases daybook to the purchases account in the ledger debit (left-hand) side (see Example 2).

Purchases Daybook   PDB2

Date	Invoice no.	Account to be credited	F	Total	VAT
19__				£ p	£ p
Aug. 1	128	Fish Bros.	L1	21.60	

Dr.   Fish Bros (A/C no. 1)   Cr.

Date	Details	F	£	p	Date	Details	F	£	p
					19__				
					Aug. 1	Purchases	PDB2	21	60

At the end of each month the purchases daybook is totalled and the total debited to the purchases account in the ledger. It will follow, therefore, that if the personal account of each supplier is credited with the value of goods supplied, and the purchases account is debited with the total purchases, then the total debits will equal the total credits, thus completing the double-entry system.

Example 2

Invoices from the following suppliers were received by the Clyde Hotel (see below).

19__			Invoice no.	£
Aug.	1	Fish Bros	128	21.60
	2	A. Wine Co. Ltd	3214	51.21
	4	A. Butcher and Sons	27	52.50
	7	A. Wine Co. Ltd	3250	32.70
	12	Fish Bros	130	42.60
	21	A. Butcher and Sons	34	63.20
	24	A. Suppliers Ltd	013	122.90
	28	A. Suppliers Ltd	016	54.00

Purchases Daybook   PDB2

Date		Invoice no.	Account to be credited	F	£ p	VAT £ p
19__						
Aug.	1	128	Fish Bros	L1	21.60	
	2	3214	A. Wine Co. Ltd	L2	51.21	
	4	27	A. Butcher and Sons	L3	52.50	
	7	3250	A. Wine Co. Ltd	L2	32.70	
	12	130	Fish Bros	L1	42.60	
	21	34	A. Butcher and Sons	L3	63.20	
	24	013	A. Suppliers Ltd	L4	122.90	
	28	016	A. Suppliers Ltd	L4	54.00	
			Purchases A/C Dr.	L5	440.71	

The postings to the ledger accounts are as follows.

Dr.   Fish Bros (A/C no. 1)   Cr.

Date	Details	F	£	p	Date	Details	F	£	p
19__					19__				
Aug. 7	Returns	RDB2	3	20	Aug. 1	Purchases	PDB2	21	60
					12	Purchases	PDB2	42	60

Dr.   A. Wine Co. Ltd (A/C no. 2)   Cr.

Date	Details	F	£	p	Date	Details	F	£	p
19__					19__				
Aug. 12	Returns	RDB2	3	36	Aug. 2	Purchases	PDB2	51	21
					7	Purchases	PDB2	32	70

Dr.   A. Butcher and Sons (A/C no. 3)   Cr.

Date	Details	F	£	p	Date	Details	F	£	p
19__					19__				
Aug. 31	Returns	RDB2	2	00	Aug. 4	Purchases	PDB2	52	50
					21	Purchases	PDB2	63	20

Dr.   A. Supplier Ltd (A/C no. 4)   Cr.

Date	Details	F	£	p	Date	Details	F	£	p
					19_ _				
					Aug.24	Purchases	PDB2	122	90
					28	Purchases	PDB2	54	00

Dr.   Purchases (A/C no. 5)   Cr.

Date	Details	F	£	p	Date	Details	F	£	p
19_ _ .									
Aug. 31	Total purchases	PDB2	440	71					

4.3   PURCHASES RETURNS (RETURNS OUT)

If for any reason goods are returned to a supplier, or if there has been an overcharge on an invoice, the supplier will then forward to the customer a credit note for the amount involved. In the accounts system credit notes are dealt with as follows:

1. The credit note (Fig. 4.2) is entered into the purchases returns daybook (returns out) (see Example 3).
2. The total amount of the credit note is posted from the purchases returns daybook to the debit (left-hand) side of the supplier's account in the ledger, as was shown in Example 2.
3. At the end of the month the total of all credit notes is posted from the purchases returns daybook to the purchases returns account in the ledger, thus completing the double-entry system (see Example 3).

Example 3

During the month of August the Clyde Hotel received the following credit notes from suppliers.

			£
Aug. 7		Fish Bros, credit note 021	3.20
12		A. Wine Co. Ltd, credit note 106	3.36
31		A. Butcher and Sons, credit note 33	2.00

Purchases Returns Daybook (Returns Out)   RDB2

Date	Credit note	Account to be debited	Folio	£ p	VAT £ p
Aug. 7	021	Fish Bros	L1	3.20	
12	106	A. Wine Co. Ltd	L2	3.36	
31	33	A. Butcher and Sons	L3	2.00	
		Purchases returns A/C Cr.	L6	8.56	

Dr.   Purchases Returns (Returns Out) (A/C no. 6)   Cr.

Date	Details	F	.	£	p	Date	Details	F	£	p
						19_ _				
						Aug. 31	Total returns	RDB2	8	56

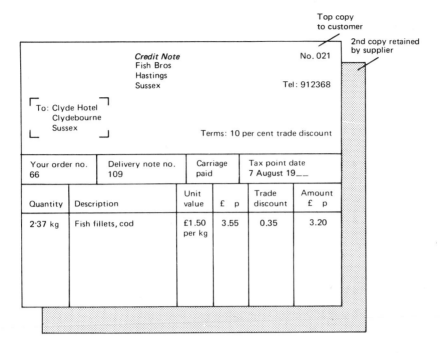

Figure 4.2   *A credit note from a supplier.*

4.4   ANALYSED PURCHASES DAYBOOK

Many hotels like to have an analysed record of their purchases so that they can keep control over the amounts spent on each type of commodity. The simplest method is to rule columns in the purchases daybook (see over) and returns daybook. The total of the invoice is still posted to the supplier's account in the ledger, and the monthly totals are posted to the purchases and purchases returns accounts, but the hotelier or restaurateur will also have a record of the amount spent on each commodity.

4.5   SUPPLIERS' MONTHLY STATEMENTS

At the end of the month a supplier will usually send a statement to the customer showing the balance owing at the beginning of the month, plus invoices for goods sent during the month, less any credit notes or monies paid (see Chapter 1). If the customer pays promptly and is entitled to receive a cash discount then the cheque and the discount received are entered into the cash payments book (see Chapter 3), and are then posted to the debit (left-hand) side of the creditor's account.

Analysed Purchases Daybook

Date	Invoice no.	Supplier	F	Total	Meat	Fish	Poultry	Dry goods	Greengrocery	Milk and bread	Wines and spirits
19__ Aug. 1	128	Fish Bros	L1	21.60		21.60					
2	3214	A. Wine Co. Ltd.	L2	51.21							51.21
4	27	A. Butcher and Sons	L3	52.50	35.00		17.50				
7	3250	A. Wine Co. Ltd.	L2	32.70							32.70
12	130	Fish Bros	L1	42.60		42.60					
21	34	A. Butcher and Sons	L3	63.20	51.20		12.00				
24	013	A. Supplier Ltd	L4	122.90				122.90			
28	016	A. Supplier Ltd	L4	54.00				54.00			
			L/5	440.71	86.20	64.20	29.50	176.90			83.91

To cross-check, the sum of these totals should add up to the amount in the total column

Example 4

19_ _

Aug. 20   The Clyde Hotel paid the amount owing at this date to A. Wine Co. Ltd, after taking a 5 per cent cash discount for prompt payment.

Cash Payments Book   CB2

Date	Details	F	Discount received	Cash	Bank
19_ _					£
Aug. 20	A. Wine Co. Ltd	L2	4.03		76.52

Dr.   A. Wine Co. Ltd (A/C no. 2)   Cr.

Date	Details	F	£	p	Date	Details	F	£	p
Aug. 12	Returns	RDB2	3	36	Aug. 2	Purchases	PDB2	51	21
20	Cash	CB2	76	52	7	Purchases	PDB2	32	70
20	Discount	CB2	4	03					
			83	91				83	91

4.6   SALES

In the accounts system of a hotel the tabular ledger (explained in detail in Chapter 6) is virtually the sales daybook and debtors' (guests) accounts combined. The income from the sale of accommodation, food and drink is transferred daily from the tabular ledger to the monthly summary sheet and is then posted to the appropriate sales account in the ledger.

Example 5

19_ _

July   The monthly total of apartment sales for the Clyde Hotel amounted to £10 500

Monthly Summary Sheet

Date	Apartments	Board	Early morning teas	Lunch	Afternoon teas	Dinner	etc.	VAT
19_ _	£ p							
July 1	350.00							
2	286.00							
3	240.00							
etc.								
Total	10 500.00							
	L20							

Dr.   Sales: Apartments (A/C no. 20)   Cr.

Date	Details	F	£	p	Date	Details	F	£	p
19_ _					19_ _				
					July 31	Monthly total	MSS	10 500	00

4.7 CASH SALES

In the recording of cash sales, where the cash is paid directly into the bank immediately after completing the transaction, the double entry is fulfilled by:

1. Debiting the amount of sales in the cash receipts book.
2. Crediting the amount of sales in the sales account in the ledger.

Example 6

19_ _
Aug. 5   The cash sales of £350 from the restaurant of the Clyde
Hotel were paid directly into the bank

CB2   Cash Receipts Book

Date	Details	F	Cash	Bank	
19__ Aug. 5	Restaurant cash sales banked	L21		350.00	

Dr.   Sales: Restaurant (A/C no. 21)   Cr.

Date	Details	F	£	p	Date	Details	F	£	p
					19_ _ Aug. 5	Cash sales	CB2	350	00

4.8 CREDIT SALES

Often hotels have customers in their restaurants who, though not residing in the hotel, wine and dine in the restaurants on a regular basis. In these cases the hotel may grant credit facilities to these customers by which, instead of paying cash immediately for their meals, they sign a waiter's check or restaurant bill which is in duplicate: the top copy the customer keeps, while the second copy is sent to the accounts section, where all bills for credit sales are entered into a subsidiary book called the restaurant sales daybook, and from there the amounts are debited to the customer's personal account in the debtors ledger. The total of the restaurant sales daybook is credited at the end of each month to the appropriate account in the ledger.

Example 7

The restaurant at the Clyde Hotel was frequently used by executives of local businesses who charged their meals to their companies' accounts with the hotel. During the month of August the following signed waiter's checks were received in the accounts section.

		£
19__		
Aug. 7	Bill no. 37 Winter Glass Co.	33.00
14	Bill no. 53 A. Summer Ltd	42.00
14	Bill no. 67 Winter Glass Co.	21.00
20	Bill no. 74 A. Summer Ltd	39.00

		£
Aug. 20	Bill no. 76 C. Breezy Ltd	18.00
24	Bill no. 84 C. Breezy Ltd	24.00
31	Bill no. 102 Winter Glass Ltd	52.00

At the end of the month the hotel sends a statement to each debtor showing the amount owing. When payment is made the cash book is debited and the customer's account credited.

Restaurant Sales Daybook   SDB2

Date	Bill no.	Account to be debited	Folio	£ p
19__				
Aug. 7	37	Winter Glass Co.	L12	33.00
14	53	A. Summer Ltd	L13	42.00
14	67	Winter Glass Co.	L12	21.00
20	74	A. Summer Ltd	L13	39.00
20	76	C. Breezy Ltd	L14	18.00
24	84	C. Breezy Ltd	L14	24.00
31	102	Winter Glass Co.	L12	52.00
31		Restaurant sales A/C Cr.	L21	229.00

Dr.   Winter Glass Co. (A/C no. 12)   Cr.

Date	Details	F	£	p	Date	Details	F	£	p
19__									
Aug. 7	Bill no. 37	SDB2	33	00					
14	Bill no. 67	SBD2	21	00					
31	Bill no. 102	SDB2	52	00					

Dr.   A. Summer Ltd (A/C no. 13)   Cr.

Date	Details	F	£	p	Date	Details	F	£	p
19__									
Aug. 14	Bill no. 53	SDB2	42	00					
20	Bill no. 74	SDB2	39	00					

Dr.   C. Breezy Ltd (A/C no. 14)   Cr.

Date	Details	F	£	p	Date	Details	F	£	p
19__									
Aug. 20	Bill no. 76	SDB2	18	00					
24	Bill no. 84	SDB2	24	00					

Dr.   Sales: Restaurant (A/C no. 21)   Cr.

Date	Details	F	£	p	Date	Details	F	£	p
					19__				
					Aug. 31	Total credit sales	SDB2	229	00

4.9 SPECIAL FUNCTIONS

When a hotel can offer facilities for special functions such as wedding receptions, luncheons, dinners or banquets, special prices are quoted and other details arranged. Payment is usually made after the event, so they are in effect credit sales and are dealt with as such in the accounts system. The management like to know exactly how much income is derived from special functions so it is customary to keep a special functions daybook and post from there to either a composite functions debtors account or individual personal debtors accounts in the ledger.

Example 8

During the month of August the following special functions were held at the Clyde Hotel.

19_ _

Aug. 7   Bill 036 Rotary luncheon for 30 at £4.50 per cover; liquors and tobacco £25. Account to B. Chase, Secretary.

     15   Bill 042 private dinner party for 12 at £8.50 per cover; liquors and tobacco £15. Account to C. Hare.

     18   Bill 055 wedding buffet for 60 at £5.50 per cover; liquors and tobacco £65. Account to B. Hound.

     28   Bill 062 Sailing Club dinner for 55 at £6.50 per cover; liquors and tobacco £50. Account to A. Field, Secretary.

Special Functions Daybook   FDB2

Date	Bill no.	Account to be debited	Folio	Food	Liquors and tobacco	Sundry extras	Total
19_ _							
Aug. 7	036	Rotary Club: 30 x £4.50 A/C to B. Chase, Sec.	L24	135.00	25.00		160.00
15	042	Private dinner party: 12 x £8.50 A/C to C. Hare	L24	102.00	15.00		117.00
18	055	Wedding buffet: 60 x £5.50 A/C to B. Hound	L24	330.00	65.00		395.00
28	062	Sailing Club dinner: 55 x £6.50 A/C to A. Field, Sec.	L24	357.50	50.00		407.50
				924.50	155.00		1079.50
				L25	L26		

Dr.   Special Functions (A/C no. 24)   Cr.

Date	Details	F	£	p	Date	Details	F	£	p
19_ _									
Aug. 7	036 Rotary Club	FDB2	160	00					
15	042 C. Hare, Private	FDB2	117	00					
18	055 B. Hound, Wedding	FDB2	395	00					
28	062 Sailing Club	FDB2	407	50					

Dr.   Sales: Functions (Food) (A/C no. 25)   Cr.

Date	Details	F	£	p	Date	Details	F	£	p
					19_ _				
					Aug. 31	Total credit sales	FDB2	924	50

Dr.   Sales: Functions (Liquor) (A/C no. 26)   Cr.

Date	Details	F	£	p	Date	Details	F	£	p
					19_ _				
					Aug. 31	Total credit sales	FDB2	155	00

Whether separate accounts are kept for sales of food at functions and for sales of liquors and tobacco at functions will depend on how much analysis of their sales the management require. The monthly total of the special functions daybook can be posted direct to one sales account in the ledger, as shown opposite.

Dr.   Special Functions Sales   Cr.

Date	Details	F	£	p	Date	Details	F	£	p
					19_ _				
					Aug. 31	Total function sales	FDB2	1079	50

When the account for the function is settled the cash book is debited with the amount and the composite special functions account is credited. The special functions account may be replaced by individual accounts for each client.

4.10 CONTROL ACCOUNTS

A control account is constructed to enable separate sections of the ledger, e.g. purchases and sales (debtors and creditors) ledgers, to be checked for accuracy. This account forms no part of the double-entry system and is simply a device to save time and localize errors in these sections.

Construction of a purchase ledger control account

1. The balance at the beginning of the month is the agreed total of the creditors' balances carried down from the previous month's control account.
2. The total purchases for the month (obtained from the daybook) is posted to the credit side of the control account.
3. The total cash and discount paid to creditors (obtained from the cash book) during the month is posted to the debit side of the control account.
4. The total of purchases returns (returns out) (obtained from the returns daybook) is posted to the debit side of the control account.
5. The account is balanced and the balance brought down to the beginning of next month's control account.
6. The balance should be equal to the total of the creditors' balances outstanding (total creditors).

Dr.   Purchases Control Account   Cr.

Date	Details	F	£	p	Date	Details	F	£	p
19_ _					19_ _				
Jan. 31	Cash	CB	5 510	00	Jan. 1	Balance (total creditors)		5 000	00
31	Discounts	CB	290	00	31	Total purchases	PDB	7 000	00
31	Returns	RDB	120	00					
31	Balance	c/d	6 080	00					
			12 000	00				12 000	00
					Feb. 1	Balance*	b/d	6 080	00

* Feb. 1: The balance should be equal to the total of the creditors' balances at this date.

Construction of a sales ledger control account

The sales control account is constructed in the same way as the purchases control account. Total debtors' balances carried down from the previous month and total credit sales are on the debit side (left-hand side) of the account, and cash discount allowed and allowances are on the credit side. The account is balanced and the balance brought down to the next month's control account. This balance should be equal to the total of the debtors' balances (total debtors). If the balances do not agree with the total creditors' or debtors' balances then errors have been made in these sections of the ledger.

Dr.   Sales Control Account   Cr.

Date	Details	F	£	p	Date	Details	F	£	p
19_ _					19_ _				
Jan. 1	Balance		600	00	Jan. 31	Cash	CB	778	00
	(total debtors)				31	Discount	CB	42	00
31	Total credit sales	SDB	890	00		Allowances	AB	20	00
						Balance	c/d	650	00
			1490	00				1490	00
Feb. 1	Balance*	b/d	650	00					

*The balance should be equal to the total of debtors' balances at this date.

4.11   VALUE ADDED TAX

VAT was first introduced in the United Kingdom in 1973 and is a tax levied on most goods and services. Certain exceptions, such as exports, food, books, newspapers, educational services, banking, doctors and dental services, are classified as zero-rated and therefore no VAT is chargeable. There are two basic rates of VAT, the standard rate and the special rate. The percentage charged can be varied at any time by the Government and since 1973 the standard rate has changed from 10 per cent to 8 per cent to 15 per cent.

The law requires that accurate records be kept of VAT output, which is that tax collected from customers, and VAT input, which is that tax payable on goods from suppliers, and HM Customs and Excise officers have the authority to inspect these records at any time.

As the VAT percentage can change at any time the basic arithmetical calculation, whatever the percentage, should be clearly understood. If a price is quoted as exclusive of VAT, that means that VAT at the current rate must be added to the price quoted. For example:

Bill	£4.00
Add 15 per cent VAT	60
Bill plus VAT	£4.60

Hoteliers and caterers are required to quote their prices as VAT inclusive, which means that the value added tax is included in the price. Therefore the tax due to the Customs and Excise must be extracted from the price quoted. If VAT is at 15 per cent the calculation would be:

Bill (100%) + VAT (15%) = VAT Inclusive Price (115%)

$$\text{Bill}\left(\frac{100^{20}}{115_{23}}\%\right) + \text{VAT}\left(\frac{15^3}{115_{23}}\right) = \frac{23}{23} \text{ (the whole)}$$

Therefore to extract the VAT from a VAT-inclusive price one must calculate $\frac{3}{23}$ by multiplying by 3 and dividing by 23. For example:

Bill (VAT inclusive)	£4.60
	×3
	13.80 ÷ by 23 = £0.60

Check:

Bill (VAT exclusive) =	£4.00
Add 15 per cent VAT	60
	£4.60

4.12 SERVICE CHARGE

Any service charge added to a bill is subject to VAT. Therefore if a price is quoted as service charge and VAT included, then to extract both the service charge and VAT the calculation would be:

Bill (VAT 15 per cent and service charge 12½ per cent included)	£41.40
Less VAT at 15 per cent (3/23)	5.40
	£36.00

Less service charge at 12½ per cent

$$\left(\frac{12.5}{112.5} = \frac{1}{9} \text{ so divide by 9} \right)$$ 4.00

Bill (VAT and service charge excluded) £32.00

To check the answer:

Bill (VAT and service charge excluded)	£32.00
Add service charge at 12½ per cent	4.00
	£36.00
Add VAT at 15 per cent	5.40
Bill (VAT and service charge included)	£41.40

4.13 ACCOUNTING FOR VAT (VALUE ADDED TAX)

In the hotel and catering industry VAT output is chargeable on the provision of meals and accommodation at the standard rate. For any period after the first four weeks of a stay at a hotel the VAT would be charged at a reduced rate.

Food purchases are zero-rated but alcoholic beverages, minerals, confectionery and certain other items are subject to VAT input tax. Purchase of equipment, repairs, telephone accounts, etc. are also subject to VAT.

To record VAT output an additional column can be added to the monthly summary sheet (see section 4.6) and posted from there to the HM Customs and Excise account in the ledger (see over). To record VAT input an additional column can be added to the purchases daybook and the purchases returns book and the monthly balance transferred to HM Customs and Excise account in the ledger, as shown.

If the VAT output exceeds the VAT input the difference is payable to HM Customs and Excise. If the VAT input exceeds the VAT output HM Customs and Excise will refund the difference.

HM Customs and Excise A/C

Date	VAT input	F	£ p	Date	VAT output	F	£ p
19__	Jan.		100.00	19__	Jan.		200.00
	Feb.		200.00		Feb.		300.00
	March		200.00		March		400.00
	Tax paid to						
	Customs and Excise	CB	400.00				
			900.00				900.00
	April		250.00		April		300.00
	May		450.00		May		350.00
	June		400.00		June		350.00
					Tax refunded by		
					Customs and Excise		100.00
			1100.00				1100.00

ASSIGNMENTS

A4.1   Distinguish between cash purchases and credit purchases.

A4.2   During the month of September 19_ _ the following invoices and credit notes were received by the Clyde Hotel from their suppliers. (It is assumed that there were no balances outstanding on 1 September 19_ _.) Write up the purchases daybook and the purchases returns book and post to the appropriate conventional ledger accounts. Also show the same accounts posted to ledger cards.

19_ _			£
Sept. 3	A. Wine Co. Ltd	Inv. 3560	124.50
6	Fish Bros	Inv. 220	56.30
8	A. Butcher and Sons	Inv. 47	37.20
12	A. Butcher and Sons	Inv. 62	48.50
14	A. Wine Co. Ltd	Inv. 3572	45.70
15	Fish Bros	Inv. 244	39.80
17	A. Wine Co. Ltd	Inv. 3588	29.50
17	A. Butcher and Sons	Credit note 15	5.20
18	A. Wine Co. Ltd	Credit note 066	12.30
21	Fish Bros	Credit note 3	2.60
23	Fish Bros	Inv. 262	44.90
25	A. Wine Co. Ltd	Credit note 072	3.00
28	A. Butcher and Sons	Inv. 73	53.20

Post totals to the purchases account and the purchases returns account, balance the creditors' accounts, and continue entering the October invoices, credit notes and cash payments in the correct books of first entry and post to the ledger accounts (ledger cards), balancing again at 31 October.

19_ _			£
Oct. 1	Fish Bros	Inv. 271	38.30
3	A. Wine Co. Ltd	Inv. 3621	102.60
4	Paid A. Butcher and Sons amount owing on 1 Oct. less 5 per cent cash discount		
7	A. Wine Co. Ltd	Credit note 088	5.20
8	A. Butcher and Sons	Inv. 82	55.40
8	Fish Bros	Inv. 278	32.10
10	Paid A. Wine Co. Ltd amount owing on 1 Oct. less 5 per cent cash discount		
12	A. Butcher and Sons	Inv. 86	22.80
15	Fish Bros	Credit note 7	2.00
17	A. Wine Co. Ltd	Inv. 3660	42.00
20	Paid Fish Bros amount owing on 1 Oct. less 5 per cent cash discount		
22	Fish Bros.	Inv. 290	36.30

Oct.	25	A. Wine Co. Ltd	Inv. 3720	66.00
	28	A. Butcher and Sons	Credit note 24	4.50

A4.3   During the month of September the following signed waiter's checks were received in the accounts office of the Clyde Hotel. Enter the bills in the restaurant sales daybook and post to the debtors' accounts in the ledger. The balances of the debtors' accounts on 1 September showed:

		£
Account no. 12 Winter Glass Co.	Balance b/d	106
Account no. 13 A. Summer Ltd	Balance b/d	81
Account no. 14 C. Breezy Ltd	Balance b/d	42

Checks:

			£
Sept.	4	Bill no. 105 C. Breezy Ltd	36.50
	5	Bill no. 121 Winter Glass Co.	11.75
	8	Bill no. 137 C. Breezy Ltd	18.30
	12	Bill no. 141 Winter Glass Co.	21.60
	15	Bill no. 143 A. Summer Ltd	34.40
	17	Bill no. 172 C. Breezy Ltd	14.10
	17	Bill no. 173 A. Summer Ltd	22.80
	18	Bill no. 175 Winter Glass Co.	10.50
	19	Bill no. 201 A. Summer Ltd	9.30
	21	Cheques were received from Winter Glass Co., A. Summer Ltd and C. Breezy Ltd for amounts owing on 1 September less 2½ per cent cash discount for prompt payment. Enter these cheques and discount allowed in the cash receipts book and post to the ledger accounts.	
	22	Allowances were given for an overcharge to:	
		Winter Glass Co.	3.00
		A. Summer Ltd	5.20
		C. Breezy Ltd	4.80
		(Post these direct to ledger accounts. Total would be debited to allowances account.)	
	24	Bill no. 220 C. Breezy Ltd	17.50
	27	Bill no. 234 Winter Glass Co.	25.70
	30	Bill no. 240 A. Summer Ltd	14.20
		Total restaurant sales daybook and post to the ledger account; balance all debtors' ledger accounts as at 30 September.	

A4.4   During the month of September the following functions were held at the Clyde Hotel. Write up the special functions daybook and post to a composite functions account in the ledger, and also show the totals as posted to the functions (food) and functions (liquor and tobacco) accounts in the ledger.

19_ _

Sept. 5   Annual dinner of the Tartan Sports Club, 60 covers at £9.50; wines and tobacco £98. Account to secretary. Bill no. 064.

9   Wedding reception for 80 covers at £7.50; wines and tobacco £75. Account to Mr Cameron. Bill no. 065.

12   Luncheon for the Rotary Club, 35 covers at £5.50; wines and tobacco £25. Account to M. Fife, Secretary. Bill no. 066.

15   Private birthday party for 30 covers at £6.00; wines and tobacco £20. Account to Mr B. Dundee. Bill no. 067.

19   Buffet luncheon for local Chamber of Commerce members, 25 covers at £5.50; wines and tobacco £25. Account to secretary. Bill no. 068.

25   Wedding reception for £55 covers at £8.00; wines and tobacco £50. Account to Mr C. Glasgow. Bill no. 069.

These accounts were all settled by 30 September. Show in the cash book the entries of the cash received less 5 per cent discount allowed for prompt payment, and post from the cash receipts book to the composite special functions account in the ledger.

A4.5   (a) From the following information prepare a purchases control account for the month of October:

		£
Oct. 1	Total creditors' balances	620.00
31	Total monthly purchases	1230.00
31	Total returns for the month of October	75.00
31	Total cash paid to creditors	798.00
31	Total discounts received	42.00

(b) From the following information prepare a sales control account for the month of October:

		£
Oct. 1	Total debtors' balances	420.00
31	Total cash receipts from debtors	302.00
31	Total discounts allowed	18.00
31	Total credit sales for October	550.00
31	Total allowances for October	22.00

A4.6   The Willow Hotel commenced business with capital of £250 000 at the bank and £4000 in cash on 1 June 19__. Transactions for the month of January were as follows:

		£
June 1	Paid by cheque for freehold premises	175 000
1	Paid by cheque for kitchen equipment	15 000
1	Paid by cheque for fixtures and fittings	25 000
1	Paid by cheque for china, plate and cutlery	7 000
6	Received invoices from suppliers:	
	S. Oak Ltd	420
	T. Ash Ltd	330
	V. Ivy Ltd	260
6	Paid wages by cash	300

June	6	Cash sales	600
	8	Paid insurance by cheque	170
	10	Paid sundry expenses by cash	50
	10	Cash sales	420
	12	Received invoices from suppliers:	
		S. Oak Ltd	240
		T. Ash Ltd	180
		V. Ivy Ltd	340
	13	Paid wages by cash	350
	14	Cash sales	900
	15	Paid into bank	1 000
	17	Received invoices from suppliers:	
		S. Oak Ltd	90
		T. Ash Ltd	120
		V. Ivy Ltd	80
	19	Cash sales	1 200
	20	Paid wages by cash	350
	21	Received credit notes from suppliers:	
		S. Oak Ltd	15
		T. Ash Ltd	27
		V. Ivy Ltd	13
	24	Paid sundry expenses by cash	25
	25	Cash sales	1 250
	27	Paid wages by cash	360
	31	Paid into bank	2 000

You are required to write up the books of first entry, post to the ledger accounts and extract a trial balance as at 30 June 19__ . From the trial balance prepare a trading, profit and loss account and balance sheets as at 30 June 19__ . Stock at end £500.

A4.7   Complete the following tables:

VAT-inclusive bill	VAT at 15 per cent	Total	Service charge at 12½ per cent	VAT-exclusive bill
£ p	£ p	£ p	£ p	£ p
13.62				
48.34				
104.80				
566.28				
5.78				
99.24				
83.06				
45.08				
12.40				
7.98				
Totals				

VAT-inclusive bill	VAT at 15 per cent	Total	Service charge at 12½ per cent	VAT-exclusive bill
£ p	£ p	£ p	£ p	£ p
10.68				
4.25				
22.16				
40.75				
128.21				
67.55				
81.93				
47.83				
33.66				
85.25				
Totals				

5 The General Journal

The general journal may be defined as a book of first entry in which transactions of an extraordinary nature are entered in chronological order. These may be:

1. Opening entries.
2. The purchase or sale of fixed assets on credit.
3. Correction of errors.
4. Closing entries.
5. Miscellaneous entries.

A journal entry consists of three parts:

1. A debit entry.
2. A credit entry.
3. Narration. This is a short note of explanation commencing with the word 'being'.

The ruling of a journal is shown below.

J1

Date	Details	Ledger folio	Debit	Credit

5.1 OPENING JOURNAL ENTRIES

When someone starts a business, in order to open up a set of books based on the double-entry book-keeping system, he or she must make a list of the assets and a list of the liabilities, find the capital (which is the difference between the assets and the liabilities) and make an opening journal entry.

Example 1

On 1 January 19_ _ the owners of the Anchor Hotel commenced business with the following assets and liabilities:

	£
Freehold premises	200 000
Fixtures and fittings	30 000
Kitchen equipment	15 000
China, glass and cutlery	3 000
Linen	750
Cash at bank	3 200
Cash in hand	150
Creditors, Ship and Co.	1 200

The opening journal entry of the Anchor Hotel would be as follows:

J1

Date	Details	Folio	Debit	Credit
			£	£
19_ _				
Jan. 1	Freehold premises	L1	200 000.00	
	Fixtures and fittings	L2	30 000.00	
	Kitchen equipment	L3	15 000.00	
	China, glass and cutlery	L4	3 000.00	
	Linen	L5	750.00	
	Cash at bank	L6	3 200.00	
	Cash in hand	L7	150.00	
	Creditor, Ship and Co.	L8		1 200.00
	Capital	L9		250 900.00
	Being assets and liabilities at this date		252 100.00	252 100.00

5.2 POSTING FROM JOURNAL TO LEDGER ACCOUNTS

1. All debit entries in the journal are posted on the debit side (left-hand side) of the accounts named, the word 'balance' being used.
2. All credit entries in the journal are posted to the credit side (right-hand side) of the accounts named, the word 'balance' being used.
3. The ledger account number will be entered in the folio column of the journal.
4. The journal folio number (page number) will be entered in the folio column of the accounts named.
5. It will follow that the total debits posted to the accounts will equal the total credits posted to the accounts and the double-entry system will be completed.

Dr. Freehold Premises (A/C no. 1) Cr.

Date	Details	F	£	p	Date	Details	F	£	p
19_ _									
Jan. 1	Balance	J1	200 000	00					

Dr. Fixtures and Fittings (A/C no. 2) Cr.

Date	Details	F	£	p	Date	Details	F	£	p
19_ _									
Jan. 1	Balance	J1	30 000	00					

Dr.   Kitchen Equipment (A/C no. 3)   **Cr.**

Date	Details	F	£	p	Date	Details	F	£	p
19_ _ Jan. 1	Balance	J1	15 000	00					

Dr.   China, Glass and Cutlery (A/C no. 4)   **Cr.**

Date	Details	F	£	p	Date	Details	F	£	p
19_ _ Jan. 1	Balance	J1	3000	00					

Dr.   Linen (A/C no. 5)   **Cr.**

Date	Details	F	£	p	Date	Details	F	£	p
19_ _ Jan. 1	Balance	J1	750	00					

Dr.   Bank (A/C no. 6)   **Cr.**

Date	Details	F	£	p	Date	Details	F	£	p
19_ _ Jan. 1	Balance	J1	3200	00					

Dr.   Cash (A/C no. 7)   **Cr.**

Date	Details	F	£	p	Date	Details	F	£	p
19_ _ Jan. 1	Balance	J1	150	00					

Dr.   Creditor, Ship and Co (A/C no. 8)   **Cr.**

Date	Details	F	£	p	Date	Details	F	£	p
					19_ _ Jan. 1	Balance	J1	1200	00

Dr.   Capital (A/C no. 9)   **Cr.**

Date	Details	F	£	p	Date	Details	F	£	p
					19_ _ Jan. 1	Balance	J1	250 900	00

5.3 PURCHASE OR SALE OF FIXED ASSETS

When fixed assets are purchased or sold on credit an entry is made in the journal.

Example 2

On 1 January 19_ _ the Anchor Hotel purchased kitchen equipment valued at £500 on credit from Fit-Rite Ltd. The journal entry would be:

Debit entry.   The kitchen equipment is an asset, so the kitchen equipment account would be debited.

Credit entry.   Fite-Rite Ltd are owed the value of the kitchen equipment and therefore are creditors of the Anchor Hotel.

Narration.   Being the purchase of kitchen equipment.

General Journal   J1

Date	Details	Folio	Debit	Credit
19_ _ Jan. 1	Kitchen equipment A/C Fit-Rite Ltd A/C Being purchase of kitchen equipment	L3 L10	£ 500.00	£ 500.00

Dr.   Kitchen Equipment (A/C no. 3)   Cr.

Date	Details	F	£	p	Date	Details	F	£	p
19_ _ Jan. 1	Fit-Rite Ltd	J1	500	00					

Dr.   Fit-Rite Ltd (A/C no. 10)   Cr.

Date	Details	F	£	p	Date	Details	F	£	p
					19_ _ Jan. 1	Kitchen equipment	J1	500	00

Example 3

On 1 July the Anchor Hotel sold an old kitchen stove valued at £50 on credit to Link Ltd. The journal entry would be:

Debit entry.   Link Ltd would owe the Anchor Hotel £50 for the old kitchen stove and therefore would be a debtor of the hotel.

Credit entry.   The old kitchen stove is an asset which is leaving the hotel, so the kitchen equipment account would be credited with £50.

Narration.   Being the sale of an old stove.

General Journal   J10

Date	Details	Folio	Debit	Credit
19_ _ July 1	Link Ltd A/C Kitchen equipment A/C Being the sale of an old stove	L11 L3	£ 50.00	£ 50.00

Dr.   Link Ltd (A/C no. 11)   Cr.

Date	Details	F	£	p	Date	Details	F	£	p
19_ _ July 1	Kitchen stove	J10	50	00					

Dr.   Kitchen Equipment (A/C no. 3)   Cr.

Date	Details	F	£	p	Date	Details	F	£	p
					19_ _ July 1	Sale of old stove	J10	50	00

5.4 CORRECTION OF ERRORS

When an error has been made in posting to the ledger it is wrong to erase or cross out the incorrect posting as there would be no explanation of the reason. The correct procedure is to correct the error by a journal entry.

Example 4

On 7 January the account of Williams Co. Ltd was credited in error with £250 instead of Williamson Co. Ltd's account.

On 8 January the account of Smith Motors Ltd was debited in error with £50 instead of B. Smythe's account.

On 9 January the purchase of linen valued at £125 was debited to the purchases account instead of the linen account.

Journal

Date	Details	Folio	Debit	Credit
19_ _			£	£
Jan. 7	Williams Co. Ltd account		250.00	
	Williamson Co. Ltd account			250.00
	Being a correction of error in posting to Williams Co. Ltd for Williamson Co. Ltd			
8	B. Smythe account		50.00	
	Smith Motors Ltd account			50.00
	Being a correction of error in posting to Smith Motors Ltd for B. Smythe			
9	Linen account		125.00	
	Purchase account			125.00
	Being correction of error in posting to purchase account for linen account			

The journal entries would then be posted to the appropriate accounts in the ledger.

Example 5

On 31 March the purchases daybook had been undercast by £200 and the restaurant sales book monthly total had been posted as £5020 instead of £5200.

For this type of error only one entry is necessary in the journal, as shown below.

Journal

Date	Details	Folio	Debit	Credit
19_ _			£	£
Mar. 31	Purchases account		200.00	
	— — — — — — — — — — — — — — —			200.00
	Being total on page six of purchases daybook undercast by £200.			
	— — — — — — — — — — — — — —		180.00	
31	Restaurant sales account			180.00
	Being monthly total of restaurant sales book being posted as £5020 instead of £5200			

Example 6

On 31 March a cash discount of £10 deducted from the total of their monthly account when payment was made had been disallowed by ABC Suppliers Ltd.

Journal

Date	Details	Folio	Debit	Credit
19_ _			£	£
Mar. 31	Discount received account		10.00	
	ABC Suppliers Ltd account			10.00
	Being cash discount of £10 disallowed			

5.5   MISCELLANEOUS ENTRIES

There are often miscellaneous transfers between accounts that require an explanation, and in these circumstances a journal entry is necessary.

Example 7

On 1 July 19_ _   £50 in wine was withdrawn from stock for hospitality (entertainment for business purposes which is classified as an expense to the business).

Journal

Date	Details	Folio	Debit	Credit
19_ _			£	£
July 1	Hospitality account		50.00	
	Stock account			50.00
	Being hospitality wine for			
	business luncheon			

Example 8

On 1 July 19_ _ Wilcox Ltd, who were creditors of the hotel, accepted in part exchange an old typewriter, value £30, the amount to be debited to their account in the ledger.

Journal

Date	Details	Folio	Debit	Credit
19_ _			£	£
July 1	Wilcox Ltd		30.00	
	Office equipment account			30.00
	Being old typewriter taken in			
	part exchange by Wilcox Ltd			

5.6   CLOSING ENTRIES

At the end of the trading period, when the final accounts are prepared, the purchases, purchases returns and sales have to be transferred to the trading account, and all the balances of the expense accounts such as wages, gas, electricity, telephone, advertising and any other expenses have to be transferred to the profit and loss account. These entries are known as closing entries and the transfers are completed by means of a journal entry.

Example 9

On 31 December 19__ the following balances were extracted from the ledger accounts of the Truro Hotel:

	£
Sales	157 316
Net purchases	60 000
Gas and electricity	6 300
Printing and stationery	3 145

At the end of the trading period the journal and ledger account entries would be as follows.

Journal   J5

Date	Details	Folio	Debit	Credit
			£	£
19__ Dec. 31	Sales account Dr. Trading account Being transfer to trading account	L1	157 316	157 316
Dec. 31	Trading account Dr. Purchases account Being transfer to trading account	L2	60 000	60 000
Dec 31	Profit and loss account Dr. Gas and electricity account Being transfer to profit and loss account	L3	6 300	6 300
Dec. 31	Profit and loss account Dr. Printing and stationery Being transfer to profit and loss account	L4	3 145	3 145

Dr.   Sales (A/C no. 1)   Cr.

Date	Details	F	£	p	Date	Details	F	£	p
19__ Dec. 31	To trading account	J5	15 316	00	19__ Dec. 31	Total sales	SDB	157	316

Dr.   Purchases (A/C no. 2)   Cr.

Date	Details	F	£	p	Date	Details	F	£	p
19__ Dec. 31	Total purchases	PDB	60 000	00	19__ Dec. 31	To trading account	J5	60 000	00

Dr.   Gas and Electricity (A/C no. 3)   Cr.

Date	Details	F	£	p	Date	Details	F	£	p
19__ Dec. 31	Cash	CB	6300	00	19__ Dec. 31	To profit and loss account	J5	6300	00

Dr.   Printing and Stationery (A/C no. 4)   Cr.

Date	Details	F	£	p	Date	Details	F	£	p
19__ Dec. 31	Cash	CB	3145	00	19__ Dec. 31	To profit and loss account	J5	3145	00

ASSIGNMENTS

A5.1   Explain briefly the purpose and uses of the general journal.

A5.2   Show the opening journal entries, ascertain the capital and post to the ledger accounts the following exercises:

(a) The Dundee Hotel commenced business with the following assets and liabilities:

19_ _		£
June 1	Freehold premises	250 000
	Restaurant furniture	12 000
	Fixtures and fittings	25 000
	Kitchen equipment	15 000
	Cash in hand	250
	Cash at bank	4 500
	Creditors: Kirk and Co.	1 500
	Bray Ltd	420
	China, glass and cutlery	500

(b) The Fife Hotel commenced business with the following assets and liabilities:

19_ _		£
March 1	Loan from B. McBain	25 000
	Leasehold premises	80 000
	Fixtures and fittings	15 000
	Kitchen equipment	7 500
	Linen	400
	China, glass and cutlery	250
	Bank overdraft	1 200
	Cash in hand	120
	Creditor, B. McVey	360
	Stock in hand	300

A5.3   Show the journal entries to record the following transactions and post to the ledger accounts.

The St Andrews Hotel

Mar. 1   Bought on credit from the Glencoe Co. Ltd kitchen equipment £750

7   Sold as part exchange to the Glencoe Co. Ltd old stove £45

14   Bought new electric typewriter on credit from the McKay Co. £140

14   McKay Co. took old typewriter £30 in part exchange

15   Bought on credit from B. McTavish new office desk £80

15   Bought on credit from McLaren Ltd china, plate and cutlery £300

A5.4   Show the journal entries to correct the following errors discovered in the books of the St Andrews Hotel.

Apr. 1 B. McGregor's account was debited with £25 instead of B. Gregory's account

5 Purchases daybook was undercast by £40

17 V. Stewart's account was credited with £50 instead of V. Stone's account

17 The purchase of china and cutlery £55 had been posted to the purchases account

30 The monthly total of £45 for discounts allowed had been debited to the discounts received account

30 The monthly total of the restaurant sales daybook had been posted as £3800 instead of £3500

A5.5   Journalize the following:

June 1 The proprietors of the St Andrews Hotel withdrew wine stock value £30 for personal use

2 A letter was sent to S. McInnes disallowing him the discount of £5 which he had deducted from his account owing £100

7 When paying McKay Co. Ltd's account of £140 a discount of £7 was deducted to which the hotel was not entitled; a letter to this effect had been received

A5.6   The following balances were extracted from the accounts of the Sunset Hotel at the end of the trading period 31 March 19_ _ . Show the closing journal entries and ledger accounts after the transfers have been made.

	£
Sales	140 200
Purchases	68 000
Purchases returns	450
Postage and stationery	860
Gas and electricity	6 300
Wages	32 000

A5.7   Ascertain the capital of the Kirkcaldy Hotel as at 1 January 19_ _ from the following list of assets and liabilities. Prepare the appropriate opening journal entry to open up a set of books at that date, and post to the ledger accounts.

		£
Freehold premises		150 000
Fixtures and fittings		20 000
Kitchen equipment		12 000
China, plate and glass		2 000
Linen		800
Creditors:	A. McRay	100
	B. McKay	200
	C. McVee	150
Cash in hand		220
Cash at bank		1 300

Enter the following transactions in the books of first entry and post to the appropriate ledger accounts.

			£
Jan. 2	Bought provisions on credit from A. McRay		120
2	Bought provisions on credit from B. McKay		60
2	Bought provisions on credit from C. McVee		180
3	Returned goods to A. McRay		10
4	Paid wages in cash		120
4	Paid insurance by cheque		140
4	Bought new kitchen equipment on credit from Fit-Rite Ltd		240
5	Paid A. McRay's account owing 1 January by cheque		100
6	Cash sales		650
Stock in hand on 7 January			80

6 The Tabular Ledger

In addition to the conventional ledger (Chapter 2) it is customary, when there is no full mechanized or computerized accounting system, for hotels to record their sales to guests and sales in other departments, such as bars and restaurants, on an analysed daily sheet known as the 'tab' (tabular ledger).

The principle of the double-entry book-keeping system is fulfilled on the tab by recording all charges made to guests and sales in other departments as *debit* entries. Allowances, transfers to the conventional ledger, cash received from sales and payments made by guests are recorded as *credit* entries. At a certain time each day the tabular ledger is balanced, all debit entries are totalled, all credit entries are totalled, and the tab is balanced and closed for that day, any outstanding balances being carried forward to the next day's tab.

There are two basic types of layout for the tabular ledger – the vertical and the horizontal – and the style used will depend on the individual requirements of the hotel.

6.1 THE VERTICAL TABULAR LEDGER

This (see Fig. 6.3) is the most popular style used, as it corresponds with the usual layout of the bill presented to the guest (Fig. 6.5). The room numbers and the names of the guests occupying the rooms are written in by hand across the tab. Printed down the left-hand side is a list of all the various kinds of charges likely to be incurred by guests, including room charge, meals, liquors and sundry items. On this layout all debit entries will be recorded in the upper section and all credit entries will be recorded in the lower section of the tab.

6.2 THE HORIZONTAL TABULAR LEDGER

This alternative style of layout (see Fig. 6.2) has the list of likely charges such as room charge, meals, liquors and sundry items printed across the tab, and the room numbers and the names of the guests occupying the rooms are written vertically down the left-hand side. On this type of layout all debit entries will appear in the left-hand section and all credit entries in the right-hand section of the tab.

6.3   SOURCES OF ENTRIES

The hotel tariff provides details of charges made by the hotel for accommodation, meals and any other additional services that it provides. For the purpose of posting the correct charges on the tabular ledger and in the guest's account, the terms quoted on the tariff are broken down into separate charges for room and breakfast, lunch, afternoon tea, beverages and other sundry charges, as shown below.

Maryville Hotel

Tariff

Room and breakfast	£18.00 (inclusive of breakfast £2.00 per person)
Inclusive terms	£25.00 (inclusive of board of £10.00 per person)
Private bathroom	£5.00 per room per night
Suites	£50.00 (Total charge for two persons including breakfast)
Extra bed (child up to 12 years)	£3.00 per room per night
Early morning tea	40p per person
Luncheon (table d'hôte)	£3.75 per person
Afternoon tea	£1.20 per person
Telephone calls	7p per unit
Beverages with meals	40p per person

All prices quoted are inclusive of VAT and service charge.

Note: The prices quoted on the hotel tariff do not reflect the current charges made by hotels, but are used only as an example to illustrate the theory.

6.4   THE TRIPLE CHECKING SYSTEM

Whenever a guest incurs a charge over and above the meals and accommodation included in the terms of reservation, details of the charge have to be forwarded immediately to the billing office so that it is recorded on the tabular ledger and the guest's bill.

The most common system in use for the purpose is known as the triple checking system (Fig. 6.1), by which there are three copies of every check (sales voucher); by using carbonized paper, whatever is written on the top copy is also recorded on the second and third copies. Each department, i.e. restaurant, bars, housekeeping, room service, stillroom, etc., has its own numbered triple-check pad, often in different colours to identify the department of origin. The top copy goes to the kitchen, dispense bar or any other supply department. The second copy is usually signed by the guest on receipt of his or her order and then is sent immediately to the billing office for entry on to the tab and the guest's account. The third copy goes to the control office where eventually all three copies are married together and checked.

6.5   APARTMENT CHARGES

These charges are quoted as either room and breakfast or inclusive (en pension), which means that breakfast, lunch, afternoon tea and dinner are included in the charge. As soon as the visitor's account is opened on the tab the room rate is debited to the account for the coming

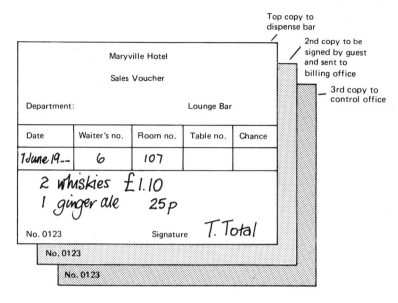

Figure 6.1   *Triple checking system.*

night's stay, and thereafter the room charge is posted to the guest's account each day before the tab is balanced and closed.

6.6   MEALS

If a guest takes any meals in addition to those included in his or her terms of residence, then a sales voucher (check) would be made out by the restaurant and forwarded to the billing office so that the charge is debited on the tab and the guest's bill.

6.7   DRINKS

Any drinks a guest may order to be charged to his or her account would be detailed on a sales voucher, a copy of which would be forwarded to the billing office, the charge to be debited on the tab and the guest's bill.

6.8   SUNDRY ITEMS

If a guest incurs any charges for sundry items such as telephone calls, laundry, valeting services, newspapers, etc. the details would be forwarded on a sales voucher to the billing office to be debited on the tab and the guest's bill. Sometimes telephones and drink vending machines are connected directly to a meter in the billing office.

6.9   DISBURSEMENTS (VISITORS' PAID-OUTS)

Very often small items of expenditure such as theatre tickets, flowers, magazines or similar sundry items are paid out of petty cash on behalf of guests. A petty cash voucher is then made out in duplicate for the disbursement and entered in the VPOs column in the petty cash book and a copy of the voucher is sent to the billing office, the disbursement to be debited on the tab and the guest's bill.

6.10   ALLOWANCES

If a guest is overcharged or given an allowance for any reason, an allowances voucher (credit note) is made out and a copy sent to the billing office, the amount of the allowance to be credited on the tab and the guest's bill.

6.11   CHANCE BUSINESS

Each day before the tab is balanced and closed, takings from cash sales in the restaurant and bars are debited separately on the tab as chance sales, the cash received from these sales being credited.

6.12   SPECIAL FUNCTIONS

If any special functions are held in the hotel, details of meals taken and drinks to be charged are debited separately on the tab. If any cash is received it is credited. If an account for the function has to be sent on, the amount involved would be credited and shown as transferred to the ledger.

6.13   DEPOSITS IN ADVANCE

When a guest has paid a deposit in advance, initially the amount would be debited in the cash received book and credited in the deposits in advance account in the conventional ledger. On the day of departure the deposit is credited to the guest's account on the tab and debited to the deposits in advance account in the conventional ledger.

6.14   TOURS AND GROUP CHARGES

Very often special rates are quoted for tour or group bookings. The billing office will have clear details of what amounts should be charged to the tour operator and what charges will be the responsibility of the individual guests. The rooms allocated to the group will be written on the tabular ledger with the names of the occupants. The word 'extras' will be written on the rate line, which means that the guests will pay separately for any sundry charges they may incur. A separate column is then opened on the tabular ledger in the name of the tour operator and the amount to be charged for the rooms and meals for the group is debited in total to that

Date: 1 Jun 19_ _

Room no.	Name	No. of guests	Terms	Balance b/f	Room charge	Board En pension	Breakfast	Early morning beverage	Lunch	Afternoon tea	Dinner	Beverages	Spirits	Liqueurs
				£ p	£ p	£ p	£ p	£ p	£ p	£ p	£ p	£ p	£ p	£ p
101	Mr B. Parson	1	Incl + Bath 30-00	78-70	20·00	10·00						0·40		
104	Mr & Mrs. R. James	2	R+B 36·00	48·00										
107	Sir, R. Pitt	1+1	R+B Bath 41·00 (43·00)	35·70	37·00		4·00					1·10		
201	Mr + Mrs. R. Carter	2	Extras	8·30										
202	Mr Mrs. L. Sales	2	Extras	20·40										
203	Mr Mrs. B. Wynn	2	Extras	22·00										
204	Mr & Mrs. M. Horton	2	Extras	10·50								0·80		
	Sun Tours Ltd		R+B	144·00	288·00									
	Chance Meals								135·00			13·60 / 4·20		
110	Mrs. M. Peacock	1	R+B 18·00		16·00		2·00		3·75					0·85
108	Mr + Mrs. G. Stone	2	Incl + Bath 55·00			35·00	20·00					0·80		
102	Mr L. Barnes	1	R+B 18·00		16·00		2·00							
	Blue Room Suite								120·00			10·00		
	Tartan Bar												37·50	
Totals				511·60	124·00	30·00	8·00		258·75			29·80	38·60	0·85

Figure 6.2   *Maryville Hotel:*

column. If an account for the amount involved is to be sent on to the tour operator then that amount would be credited on the tab and transferred to the conventional ledger.

6.15   TABULAR LEDGER PROCEDURES

As guests can arrive or depart at any time of the day, it is essential that the tabular ledger is always up to date. Therefore all sales vouchers must be forwarded immediately to the billing office for debiting to the tab and the guests' bills, and it is common practice for a line to be put through the sales check to indicate that it has been posted. The ideal time to balance and close the tabular ledger is late evening at the close of the day's business, but if no late shift is on duty then it must be the first job in the morning.

Step-by-step routine

1. After balancing and closing the previous day's tab, room numbers, names, terms and rates of the guests in residence are entered on the new tab.
2. Balances carried forward from the previous day are entered.

Wines	Beers	Minerals	Bar-liquor	Tobacco	Telephone	Newspapers	Sundries	VPOs	Total debits	Allowances	Cash received	Transferred to ledger	c/f	Total credits	Folio no.
£ p	£ p	£ p	£ p	£ p	£ p	£ p	£ p	£ p	£ p	£ p	£ p	£ p	£ p	£ p	£ p
1·80					1·20	0·15			112·25				112·25	112·25	
						0·30		1·00	49·30	o/c 0·40		48·90		49·30	American Express
u/c 3·20		0·25			0·40			2·60	84·25				84·25	84·25	
									8·30		8·30			8·30	
									20·40		20·40			20·40	
					3·50				25·50		25·50			25·50	
									11·30		11·30			11·30	
									288·00			288·00		288·00	Sun Tours Ltd
21·00	4·80	2·20							180·80		180·80			180·80	
					0·66			1·80	25·06				25·06	25·06	
	0·55				0·80				57·15				57·15	57·15	
					0·60				18·60		20·00		(1·60)	18·60	
60·00			42·50						232·50		42·50	190·00		232·50	Ciro Ltd
	18·40	1·80		10·60					68·30		68·30			68·30	
86·00	23·75	4·25	42·50	10·60	7·16	0·45		5·40	1181·71	0·40	377·10	526·90	277·31	1181·71	

horizontal tabular ledger

3. The room numbers, names, terms and rates of any new arrivals are entered in red to indicate quite clearly that they are new arrivals.
4. If guests are departing, it must be checked that all charges have been debited on the tab and the guests' bills, and any allowances, deposits in advance or payments made have been credited. A line is put through the room number on the tab to indicate a departure. (See Fig. 6.2 and Fig. 6.3.)
5. If a guest changes his or her room for any reason the old number is crossed out and the new room number written above, both on the guest's bill and on the tab. Care must be taken to ensure that sales vouchers are posted to the correct room number.
6. At the close of business, cash takings from bars and restaurants are collated, the sales figures being debited on the tabular ledger and any cash received being credited.
7. Any special-function business is debited with details on the tab. If an account has to be sent on, then the amount would be credited and transferred to the conventional ledger.
8. Any special charges for tours, groups or other similar types of business are debited in the appropriate columns. If cash is received the amount is credited; if an account has to be sent on the amount is credited and transferred to conventional ledger.
9. Finally the room rate for each guest in residence on the coming night is debited to the tab.
10. At the close of the day's business the tabular ledger is totalled and balanced, the balances outstanding being transferred to the next day's tab.

Date 1 June 19— —

	1	2	3	4	5	6	7	8	9	10	11	12	13	14	15
Room number	101	104	107	201	202	'203	204	Sun Tours Ltd	Chance meals	110	108	102	Blue Room Suite	Tartan Bar	Totals
Name	Mr B. Anson	Mr+Mrs R. James	Sir R. Pitt	Mr+Mrs R. Carter	Mr+Mrs L. Sales	Mr+Mrs B. Wynn	Mr+Mrs M. Horton			Mrs M. Peacock	Mr+Mrs G. Stone	Mr L. Barnes			
Number of adults / Number of children	1	2	1+1	2	2	2	2			1	2	1			
Terms	Incl+ Bath	R+B	R+B Bath	Extras	Extras	Extras	Extras	R+B		R+B	Incl+ Bath	R+B			
Rate	30.00	36.00	41.00 / 23.00					144.00		18.00	55.00	18.00			
16 Balance b/f	78.70	48.00	35.70	8.30	20.40	22.00	10.50	288.00							511.60
Apartments	20.00		37.00							16.00	35.00	16.00			124.00
Board (pension)	10.00										20.00				30.00
Early morning beverages															
Breakfast			4.00							2.00		2.00			8.00
Lunch									135.00	3.75			120.00		258.75
Afternoon tea															
Dinner															
Beverages	0.40						0.80		13.60; 4.20		0.80		10.00		29.80
Spirits			1.10											37.50	38.60
Liqueurs										0.85					0.85
Wines	1.80		3.20/c						21.00				60.00		86.00
Beers									4.80		0.55			18.40	23.75
Minerals			0.25						2.20					1.80	4.25
Bar–Liquor													42.50		42.50
Tobacco etc.														10.60	10.60
Telephone	1.20		0.40			3.50				0.66	0.80	0.60			7.16
Newspapers	0.15	0.30													0.45
Sundries															
VPOs		1.00	2.60							1.80					5.40
17 Total debits	112.25	49.30	84.25	8.30	20.40	25.50	11.30	288.00	180.80	25.06	57.15	18.60	232.50	68.30	1181.71
18 Allowances		0.40													0.40
19 Cash received				8.30	20.40	25.50	11.30		180.80			20.00	42.50	68.30	377.10
20 Transferred to ledger		48.90						288.00					190.00		526.90
21 C/f	112.25		84.25							25.06	57.15	(1.40)			277.31
22 Total credits	112.25	49.30	84.25	8.30	20.40	25.50	11.30	288.00	180.80	25.06	57.15	18.60	232.50	68.30	1181.71
23 Folio no.	American Express	American Express						Sun Tours Ltd					Giro Ltd		

Figure 6.3   *Maryville Hotel: vertical tabular ledger.*

Key to Fig. 6.3, vertical tabular ledger

Column

1.	Room 101 Mr B. Parson, inclusive terms plus private bathroom £25 + £5 = £30.
2.	Room 104 Mr and Mrs R. James, room and breakfast 2 × £18 = £36. Line through room no. shows departure at 11.30 a.m.
3.	Room 107 Sir R. Pitt, room and breakfast plus private bathroom £18 + £5 = £23. (+ 1 shows Lady Pitt joined her husband and rate changed to £23 + £18 = £41.)
4, 5, 6, 7.	Rooms allocated to Sun Tours Ltd party. The word 'extras' on the rate line indicates that any extra charges incurred by these guests will be paid by them individually. Lines through the room numbers indicate departure at 11 a.m.
8.	Column created for Sun Tours Ltd, who will be responsible for the payment for room and breakfast for the party of 8 at £18 = £144 per night, the account to be transferred to the ledger.
9.	Chance meals, beverages, wines, beers and minerals debited, the cash received credited.
10, 11, 12.	New arrivals, their terms entered on arrival and in red.
13.	Column created for special function in Blue Room Suite. Sales in cash bar entered as debits, the cash received from takings entered as credits. Sales from lunches, beverages and wines entered as debits, the total being transferred to the ledger for an account to be sent on to Ciro Ltd, who will make payment.
14.	Sales of spirits, beers and minerals in the Tartan Bar entered as debits, the cash received from takings entered as credits.
15.	Each line across the tab is totalled.
16.	Balances brought forward from previous day's tab entered.
17.	The daily total and the balance brought forward are added together to equal total debits. (Total debits – balance brought forward = daily total.)
18.	Any allowances entered as credits.
19.	Any cash received entered as credits.
20.	Any accounts that have to be transferred to the ledger.
21.	Balances carried forward.
22.	Total credits.
23.	Folio no. and notes.

If all entries are correctly added, *total debits* = *total credits*.

Note. Fig. 6.5 illustrates Mr B.Parson's guest's bill to date.

Example

The following exercise is entered on both the horizontal tabular ledger (Fig. 6.2) and the vertical tabular ledger (Fig. 6.3). Study the exercise carefully and follow each transaction as it appears on both types of tab and as the totals appear on the monthly summary sheet (Fig. 6.4).

Tariff for the Maryville Hotel

Room and breakfast	£18 (inc. of breakfast £2.00 per person)
Inclusive terms	£25 (inc. of board £10 per person)
Private bathroom	£5 per night
Beverages	40p per person
Luncheon	£3.75 per person

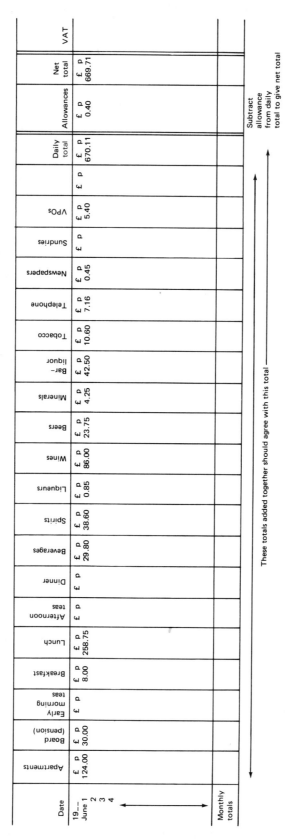

Figure 6.4 *Monthly summary sheet.*

List of guests in residence   *Balance b/f*

                                                                                 £

Room 101   Mr B. Parson   inc. with bath   78.70
Room 104   Mr and Mrs R. James   Room and breakfast   48.00
Room 107   Sir R. Pitt   Room with bath and   35.70
                                       breakfast
Rooms 201–   Sun Tours Ltd   Sun Tours Ltd pay   288.00
   204   for room and break-
   inc.   fast only and mem-
                                        bers of party pay for
                                        any extras
Room 201   Mr and Mrs R. Carter   extras   8.30
     202   Mr and Mrs L. Sales   extras   20.40
     203   Mr and Mrs B. Wynn   extras   22.00
     204   Mr and Mrs M. Horton   extras   10.50

Maryville Hotel
Jamestown
Co. Durham
Telephone (0976 1207)

VAT reg. no. 1234560

Mr. B. Parson

Room no.101
No. of persons. 1

Date	30 May 19_ _	31 May 19_ _	1 June 19_ _	2 June 19_ _		
	£ p	£ p	£ p	£ p	£ p	£ p
b/f		42·60	78·70	112·25		
En pension	30·00	30·00	30·00			
Room & breakfast						
Early morning tea						
Breakfast	(2 Extra)					
Lunch	7·50					
Afternoon tea						
Dinner						
Beverages	0·40	0·40	0·40			
Spirits	1·40	1·40				
Liqueurs						
Wines	1·80	1·80	1·80			
Beers						
Minerals						
Tobacco						
Telephone	1·20	2·20	1·20			
Newspapers	0·30	0·30	0·15			
Sundries						
Garage						
Sub-total c/f	42·60	78·70	112·25			

VAT

Total

Less deposit

Total due

No. 125

Figure 6.5   *Example of Mr B. Parson's bill to date. (See Fig. 6.3)*

List of transactions

0730	Newspapers:
	Room 101 15p
	Room 104 30p
0745	Telephone calls Room 203 £3.50
0930	Breakfast served to all residents
0930	Disbursements Room 104 medicine £1.00
0930	Lady Pitt joins her husband in Room 107 (change rate)
1000	Morning coffee Room 204 80p
1100	Sun Tours leave; transfer main account to ledger. All members of the party settle their accounts by cash.
1115	Control office notifies you that a bottle of wine £3.20 was omitted from the luncheon bill of Room 107 yesterday; make necessary adjustments
1115	Chance coffees £4.20
1115	Arrival: Mrs M. Peacock given Room 110 terms R and B
1130	Arrival: Mr and Mrs G. Stone given Room 108 with private bathroom, terms inclusive
1130	Departure: Mr and Mrs R. James Room 104 who pay their account by American Express after an adjustment of an overcharge of 40p on yesterday's bill
1215	Room 107, two whiskies £1.10 one ginger ale 25p
1230	Chance arrival: Mr L. Barnes is given Room 102 terms R and B after paying a deposit of £20
1400	Lunches:
	Room 101 one lunch one coffee, wine £1.80
	Room 108 two lunches two coffees, beer 55p
	Room 110 one lunch one liqueur 85p
	Chance 36 lunches 34 coffees, wine £21, beers £4.80, minerals £2.20
1430	Blue Room Suite, private luncheon party £120, wine £60, coffee £10, cash bar £42.50, bill to Ciro Ltd
1500	Disbursements:
	Room 107 taxi £2.60
	Room 110 flowers £1.80
1530	Tartan Bar takings:
	Spirits £37.50
	Beers £18.40
	Minerals £1.80
	Tobacco £10.60
1600	Telephone calls:
	Room 101 £1.20
	Room 102 60p
	Room 108 80p
	Room 107 40p
	Room 110 66p

6.16 MANUAL BUSINESS SYSTEMS FOR THE SMALL HOTEL

In order to minimize the clerical work and eliminate errors made by copying, patented systems

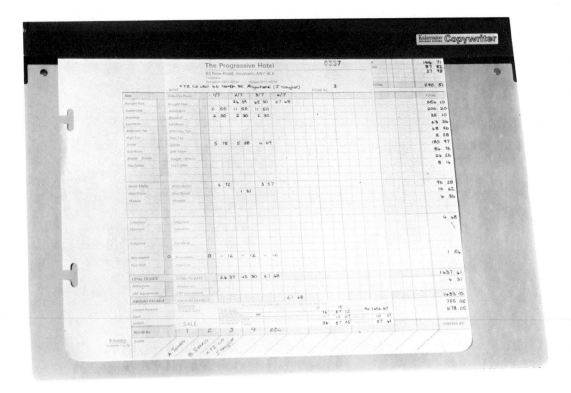

Figure 6.6 *Kalamazoo system: guest bill. Reproduced with the permission of Kalamazoo Business Systems.*

have been specially designed to help the small hotelier and guest house owner to control his or her business efficiently and obtain maximum information. There are many such systems on the market and one typical example is the Kalamazoo system, which is a collator board with studs and specially printed IDEM documents that are placed on the collator studs. Entries can then be made on all documents simultaneously, thus eliminating copying errors. The system uses three forms: the guest bill (Fig. 6.6), the tabular ledger (Fig. 6.7) and the tabular summary sheet (Fig. 6.8).

Procedure

1. Arrival. On arrival of a new guest, a guest bill (Fig. 6.6) is originated showing the guest's name and room number.
2. Billing. Throughout the day, checks and slips for various services supplied to the guest are received in the reception office. These are posted to the bill and tabular ledger (Fig. 6.7) simultaneously.
3. Posting. The tabular ledger is placed on the collator and the bill aligned over the collator studs with the next blank column on the bill being aligned with the corresponding room number on the tab, the first entry being the date and the amount brought forward.
4. Departure. When a guest is leaving his or her bill is aligned with the appropriate column on the tab. Unposted slips are entered and the bill totalled, any service charge and deposits paid being entered to arrive at the amount payable. The bill is handed to the guest and the appropriate settlement details entered on the tab.

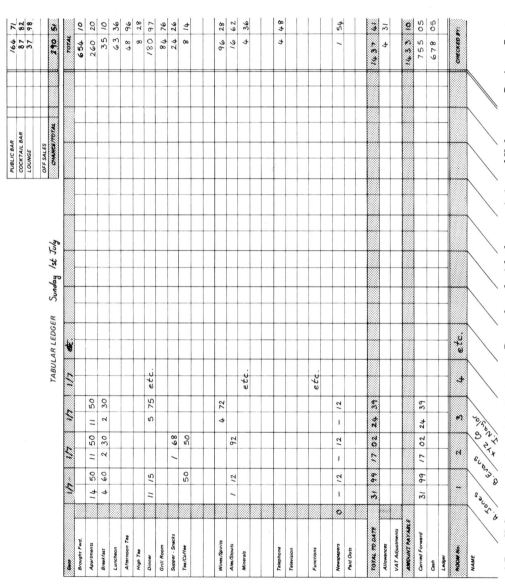

Figure 6.7   *Kalamazoo system: tabular ledger. Reproduced with the permission of Kalamazoo Business Systems.*

	1/7		2/7		3/7		4/7	5/7	6/7	7/7			Total
PUBLIC BAR	164	71	151	02									1263 15
COCKTAIL BAR	87	82	75	08									547 15
LOUNGE	37	98	31	90									273 02
OFF SALES													
CHARGE TOTAL	290	51	258	00									2084 02
Date													
Brought Fwd.	654	10	755	05	638	83							5858 09
Apartments	206	20	195	80									1860 20
Breakfast	35	10	29	90									333 80
Luncheon	63	36	57	12									602 17
Afternoon Tea	48	96	22	22	etc.								317 43
High Tea	8	28	8	28									61 57
Dinner	180	97	147	39									1359 70
Grill Room	84	76	58	41									638 30
Supper - Snacks	24	26	20	17									201 26
Tea/Coffee	8	14	7	20									59 74
Wines/Spirits	96	28	84	90									811 51
Ales/Stouts	16	62	14	19	etc.								139 49
Minerals	4	36	1	12									27 85
Telephone	4	48	5	16									23 15
Television													
Functions			50	84	etc.								50 84
Newspapers	1	54	1	24									9 16
Paid Outs													
TOTAL TO DATE	1437	41	1458	99									12354 26
Allowances	4	31											4 31
AMOUNT PAYABLE	1433	10	1458	99									12349 95
Carried Forward	755	05	638	83									5028 50
Cash	678	05	820	16									7101 35
Ledger													220 10

TABULAR LEDGER SUMMARY

Week Ending 7th July

Figure 6.8 *Kalamazoo system: tabular summary sheet. Reproduced with the permission of Kalamazoo Business Systems.*

5. Totalling and summarizing the tab:
   (a) Any chance sales are posted to the head of the tab.
   (b) Any function business is entered in the appropriate panel on the tab.
   (c) The tab is now cross-cast and proved.
   (d) If more than one tab sheet is used, the daily totals are obtained by fanning the tab sheets over the collator and adding the page totals to give a grand total on the summary sheet (Fig. 6.8).

Advantages of the system

There is less writing and no copying, as the guest's bill and the tab are completed simultaneously.

Since all cost items are pre-printed, the guest's bill is easily and promptly prepared.

The tab journals totalled, overlapped and summarized to show income and expenditure over a day, week or month provide necessary management information.

(Fig. 6.9 shows a composite booking information form and guest's bill, and Fig. 6.10 shows a Kalamazoo posting box.)

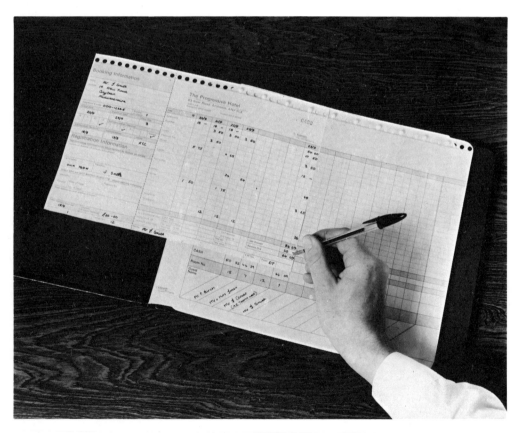

Figure 6.9   *Kalamazoo composite booking information and guest's bill. Reproduced with the permission of Kalamazoo Business Systems.*

Figure 6.10 *Kalamazoo posting box. Reproduced with the permission of Kalamazoo Business Systems.*

ASSIGNMENTS

A6.1   Describe briefly the basic differences between the vertical and the horizontal styles of tabular ledger.

A6.2   Write short notes on how the following are dealt with on the tabular ledger:

(a) deposits in advance;
(b) payment by credit card;
(c) a special function when the account has to be sent on for payment by the company on whose behalf the function has been held.

A6.3   Explain briefly the book-keeping treatment on the tabular ledger of a party of eight guests booked by Vistatours, who have been quoted a special price for room and breakfast for the group.

A6.4   (a) Enter on a visitors' tabular ledger sheet the particulars of the guests listed below, who are in residence when you come on duty in the morning.
(b) Enter all the transactions listed below.
(c) Finally, close and balance the tab as if it were at the end of the day's business, adding and reconciling all totals.

Tariff for the Bellair Hotel

Room and breakfast	£18 (inc. of breakfast £1.50 per person)
Inclusive terms	£28 (inc. of board £12 per person)
Private bathroom	£5 per night
Early morning beverages	40p per person
Afternoon tea	£1.20 per person
Coffee and other beverages served with meals	40p per person
Telephone calls	7p per unit

Note:

1. Terms are charged daily in advance, or for new arrivals immediately upon arrival.
2. Inclusive terms cover room, breakfast, lunch, afternoon tea and dinner only.
3. All prices quoted are inclusive of service charge and VAT.
4. Newspapers to be listed under VPOs.
5. Charge for suite (£50) is total charge for two people (inc. breakfast).

List of guests in residence

Name	Room no.	Room type	Terms	Balance b/f
Mr and Mrs J. Williams	101	Double with bath	R & B	£75.10
M.A. Dubois	102	Single with bath	inc.	£84.40
Mr and Mrs K. Holmes	103	Double with bath	inc.	£127.50
Misses Bell and Rolly	104/5	Singles	R & B	£68.60
Ms L. Tutt	108	Single with bath	R & B	£54.00
Mr and Mrs J. Robinson	Silver Suite		R & B	£147.95

List of transactions

0700   The night porter's record shows that the following transactions took place during the night:

        0300   Room 102 scotch (95p) and soda (25p)

        0630   Departure: Room 102 paid by cheque (cheque herewith)

0730   Early morning tea served to all residents

0800   Telephone calls Room 101 7 units

0830   Departure: Room 101 paid by cash (Note: a deposit of £50 paid in advance has not been deducted)

0900   Breakfast checks for all residents are received in the bills office

0930   Chance breakfasts £8.50

1000   Telephone calls:

        Room 103 1 unit

        Room 105 6 units

        Silver Suite 5 units

1030   Departure: Misses Bell & Rolly Rooms 104 and 105 combined account to be sent to Smith Co. Ltd, Staines

1045   Disbursements:

        Silver Suite £6.10 hairdresser

        Room 108 £2.50 chocolates

        Room 103 £2.70 taxi

1100   Morning coffee (40p per person) served to all residents

        Chance coffees £6.30

1145   Make the following allowances and adjustments to correct yesterday's tab:

        Room 103 undercharged £1 on apartments portion of inclusive terms

        Room 108 charged £2.40 for afternoon teas instead of Silver Suite

        Underpayment of chance coffees (cash herewith) £2

1200   Arrival: Mr and Mrs J. Vine Room 109 (with private bath) on inclusive terms. The account for inc. terms only to be sent to Glassware Ltd, Stoke. All other charges to be paid for separately by Mr and Mrs Vine.

        Stockrooms 4 and 5 are allocated to Glassware Ltd, Stoke, hire charge £35 per room per day

1230   Mrs Robinson pays her account up to and including yesterday by cheque

1430   The restaurant book shows the following:

Room	Luncheons	Wines	Spirits and liqueurs	Minerals	Beverages	Total
103			1.90		0.40	2.30
108	8.15	2.10		1.20	0.40	11.85
109		2.80			0.40	3.20
Silver Suite	14.50	4.50			0.80	19.80
Chance	107.75	80.70	24.10	10.00	7.50	230.05
	130.40	90.10	26.00	11.20	9.50	267.20

1530   The bars pay in the following amounts:

        Lounge bar £89.18 for liquor and £10.77 for tobacco

        Public bar £82.93 for liquor and £12.90 for tobacco

1600   Pan Suite: Luncheon for Gourmets Society. Hire of room £20, 50 lunches at £16 each, wines £84, liqueurs £22.40, cigars £20; account to be sent to Secretary of the Society in London.

A6.5 (a) Enter on a visitors' tabular ledger sheet the particulars of the guests listed below, who are in residence when you come on duty in the morning.

(b) Enter all the transactions listed below.

(c) Finally, close and balance the tab as if it were at the end of the day's business, adding and reconciling all totals.

Tariff for the Cavender Hotel

Room and breakfast	£14 (inc. of breakfast £2 per person)
Inclusive terms	£20 (inc. of board £11.50 per person)
Private bathroom	£5 per night
Extra bed (child up to 12 years)	£3 per room per night
Early morning tea	40p per person
Morning coffee	50p per person
Luncheon (table d'hôte)	£3.75 per person
Meal beverage	40p per person

Note:

1. Terms in this hotel are charged in advance, or for new arrivals immediately upon arrival.
2. Inclusive terms cover room, breakfast, lunch, afternoon tea and dinner only.
3. All prices quoted are inclusive of service charge and VAT.

List of guests in residence

Type	Terms	Room no.	Name	Balance b/f
Double with bath	R & B	112	Mr and Mrs H. Smith	£86.90
Twin	inc.	114	Mr and Mrs J. Harper	£120.20
Twin with bath	R & B	116	Miss L. Jones Miss W. Anton	£62.57
Single with bath	R & B	117	Mr S. Stewart	£42.30
Single	inc.	106	Ms E. James	£32.60

List of transactions

0700   The night porter's record shows that the following transasctions took place during the night:
0500   Large scotch and soda to Mr S. Stewart 95p
0530   Small scotch and soda to Mr S. Stewart 58p
This concludes the night porter's record.

0730   Early morning tea to all residents
Newspapers:
Room 106 40p
Room 112 20p
Room 114 40p

0745   Telephone calls:
Room 106 £3.20
Room 114 95p
Room 117 £2.55

0800   Breakfast to all residents

0820   VPOs:
Room 116 £4 taxi fare
Room 112 £5.60 cleaning
Room 106 £10 doctor

0900	Allowances and adjustments for the correction of errors in yesterday's tab:
	Room 114 not charged for three luncheon guests
	Room 117 charged 95p for phone calls instead of Room 116
	Room 112 not charged for seven morning coffee guests
0915	Departure: Mr and Mrs Harper, Room 114, paid cash less amount of £25 received as an advance deposit
0925	Chance breakfasts £24
0930	Departure: Miss Jones and Miss Anton, Room 116, signed their account which is to be charged to Opel Ltd (an advance deposit of £20 has already been paid)
0950	Mr Smith pays £75 by cheque on his account
1005	Arrival: Mr and Mrs J. Edwards arrive and are given Room 115, terms inc.
1015	Arrival: Mr and Mrs W. Jenkins and 12-year-old daughter, Jean, are given Room 215, a three-bedded room, terms R & B
1020	Mrs Jenkins pays £70 in cash on her account
1030	Arrival: Ms J. White is given Room 209 (single with bath) and pays for six nights in advance, terms R & B
1115	All residents are served with morning coffee
	Chance coffees £6.40
1300	Lunches:
	Room 209 1 lunch, wine £3.30, minerals 90p, 1 coffee
	Room 215 3 lunches, beers £1.34, minerals 80p, 2 coffees, 1 tea
	Chance: £47.50, wines £25.96, liqueurs £3.54, beverages £4.20
1400	Departure: Ms James, Room 106, is charged an additional £5 for not vacating her room by 1200; she pays cash for her account
1500	Exhibition in the Blue Suite, ABC Ltd, room hire £120, 9 lunches at £4.25 each, wine £13.58, cigars £2.33
1600	Cocktail bar pays in: beers £25.30, spirits and liqueurs £9.50, cigarettes £7.90

A6.6 (a) Enter on a visitors' tabular ledger sheet the particulars of the guests listed below, who are in residence when you come on duty in the morning.

(b) Enter all the transactions listed below in chronological order.

(c) Finally, close and balance the tab as if it were at the end of the day's business, adding and reconciling all totals.

Tariff for the Royal Hotel

Room and breakfast	£15.50 (inc. of breakfast £2.25 per person)
Inclusive terms	£21 (inc. of board £12.25 per person)
Private bathroom	£6 per room per night
Extra bed (child up to and including 14 years)	£3.50 per night exc. of meals
Early morning tea	40p per person
Coffee	50p per person
Luncheon (table d'hôte)	£4.25 per person

Note:

1. Terms are charged daily in advance, or for new arrivals immediately upon arrival.
2. Inclusive terms cover room, breakfast, lunch, afternoon tea and dinner only.

3. All prices quoted are inclusive of service charge and VAT.
4. Newspapers to be listed under VPOs.

List of guests in residence

Type	Terms	Room no.	Name	Balance b/f
Single	R & B	101	Mr R. Hurst	£63.22
Twin	R & B	103	Mr and Mrs J. Hill	£90.50
Double with bath	inc.	107	Mr and Mrs F. East	£130.40
Single with bath	inc.	110	Miss L. West	£36.70

List of transactions

0730	Early morning tea to all residents
	Newspapers:
	Room 101 40p
	Room 103 60p
	Room 107 40p
0750	Telephone calls:
	Room 103 £1.08
	Room 107 40p
	Room 110 84p
0800	Breakfast served to all residents
0835	VPOs:
	Room 101 taxis £1.95
	Room 107 flowers £4.25
0900	Allowances and adjustments for the correction of errors in yesterday's tab:
	Room 101 was charged for two luncheon guests by mistake
	Room 107 was charged for £2.25 for taxis instead of Room 110
	Room 110 omission of £2.75 for wine
0915	Chance breakfasts £11.25
0935	Departure: Mr and Mrs East, Room 107, pay by cheque less an amount of £50 received as an advance deposit
0945	Departure: Mr Hurst, Room 101, signs his account which is to be charged to Wynn Investments Ltd
0955	Miss West, Room 110, pays £30 of her account by traveller's cheque
1000	Arrival: Mr and Mrs F. Castle and 13-year old daughter, Diane, are given Room 106, a three-bedded room; terms R & B
1020	Arrival: Ms S. Simpson is given Room 112 (single) and pays for three nights in advance; terms R & B
1100	All residents are served morning coffee
1130	Chance morning coffees £4
1300	Lunches:
	Room 112 1 lunch, wine £1.75, 1 coffee
	Room 106 3 lunches, wine £2.50, minerals 70p, 2 coffees
	Room 110 1 lunch, spirits £1.45, wine £2.65, 1 coffee
	Chance lunches £46.75, wine £23.96, liqueurs £2.80, beverages £2.50
1345	Ms S. Simpson, Room 112, moves to Room 116, single with bath
1500	Trade exhibition in Rose Suite, Knight Construction Ltd; room hire £125, 10 lunches at £5.50 per person, wine £12.95, cigars and cigarettes £2.90, flowers £15.
1545	Lounge bar pays in: beers £24.40, spirits and liqueurs £7.40, cigars and cigarettes £2.90

A6.7 (a) Enter on a visitors' tabular ledger sheet the particulars of the guests listed below who are in residence when you come on duty in the morning.

(b) Enter all the transactions listed below in chronological order.

(c) Finally, close and balance the tab as if it were at the end of the day's business, adding and reconciling all totals.

Tariff for the Jamesville Hotel

Room and breakfast charge £15.25 per person per night
(allocated £12.75 to apartments and £2.50 to breakfast)
Inclusive terms £22.50 to £23.50 per person per day
(allocated £10 or £11 respectively to apartments and £12.50 to board)
Inclusive terms include afternoon tea but not coffee after meals or early
morning tea

List of guests in residence

Room no.	Name	Terms	Balance b/f
101	Mr and Mrs J. Jarvis	inc. £22.50	£87.46
102	Miss A. Curtis	inc. £23.50	£28.50
104	Capt. and Mrs R. Dean	R & B	£47.50
106	Mr and Mrs D. Everett	R & B	£41.55
107	Mr R. Pitt	inc. £22.50	£24.20
108	Mrs J. Garner	R & B	£42.25
110	Mr and Mrs A. Hinds	R & B	£50.33

List of transactions

0800   Early morning tea:
      Room 101 80p
      Room 102 40p
      Room 104 80p
      Room 106 80p
      Room 107 40p
   Newspapers:
      Room 101 20p
      Room 104 35p
      Room 106 30p
      Room 110 35p

0900   Breakfast to all residents

0930   Departures: Mr Pitt, Room 107, paid account by cash; Miss Curtis, Room 102, account transferred to ledger folio 15

0945   Disbursement: flowers for Mrs Garner, Room 108, £2.50

1000   Mr Everett, Room 106, paid £20 on account

1015   Mrs Garner transferred to Room 107

1030   Telephone charges:
      Room 104 45p
      Room 106 60p
      Room 107 75p

1100   Morning coffee:
      Room 101 80p
      Room 107 40p
      Chance £2.60
   Arrival: Mr K. Green given Room 102, terms R & B

1400   Lunches:
          Room 101 2 lunches, coffee 80p, beers 65p
          Room 102 1 lunch, coffee 40p
          Room 104, lunches £8.50, whisky 65p mineral 30p
          Room 106, lunches £8.50, coffee 80p
       Chance lunches £25.50, coffees £3.20, wines £22.40
       Spirits £7.50, beers £3.40, cigarettes £4.20
       Seattle Rotary Club luncheon, 30 lunches at £5.75, 30 coffees at 40p to
       be charged and transferred to ledger folio 18

1430   Arrival: Mr and Mrs E. Kyte given Room 103, terms £23.50 inc.

1500   Disbursement: Mrs Garner, theatre tickets £6.50

1600   Control discloses an overcharge of 30p on previous day to Room 104, an
       omission of 40p for coffee to Room 110, and £1.20 for wine charged to
       Room 106 instead of Room 104

1630   Departure: Capt. and Mrs Dean, Room 104, paid account in cash

1630   Afternoon teas:
          Room 102 £1.50
          Room 103 £1.50
          Chance £4.50

1800   Arrival: Mr F. Black given Room 112 terms £23.50 inc.

2000   Dinners:
          Room 101 2 dinners
          Room 102 dinner £6.50, coffee 40p, wine £2.75
          Room 103 2 dinners, coffee 80p
          Room 112 1 dinner, coffee 40p, wine £2.25
       Chance dinners £52, coffees £3.20, wines £15.45, liqueurs £2.70, cigars and
       cigarettes £4.35
       Banquet Room, 20 dinners at £7.50, wines £36.20, to be charged to the
       account of Ms Parry, ledger folio 22
       Cash bar £24.40

2100   Hotel bar liquors and minerals £33.40, cigarettes £10.20

A6.8   (a) Enter on a visitors' tabular ledger sheet the particulars of the guests listed below
         who are in residence when you come on duty in the morning.
    (b) Enter all the transactions listed below in chronological order.
    (c) Finally close and balance the tab as if it were at the end of the day's business,
        adding and reconciling all totals.

Tariff of the Dalton Hotel

Room and breakfast	£15 (inc. of breakfast £2 per person)
Inclusive terms	£25 (inc. of board £12.50 per person)
Private bathroom	£5 per room per night
Early morning tea	40p per person
Morning coffee	50p per person
Luncheon (table d'hôte)	£4.25 per person
Meal beverage	40p per person

Note:

1.   Terms are charged daily in advance, and for new arrivals
     immediately upon arrival.
2.   All prices quoted are inclusive of service charge and VAT.

3. Inclusive terms cover room, breakfast, lunch, afternoon tea and dinner only.

List of guests in residence

Type	Terms	Room no.	Name	Balance b/f
Double with bath	inc.	501	Mr and Mrs S. Williams	£76.70
Twin	inc.	503	Capt. and Mrs R. James	£56.47
Single with bath	R & B	504	Rev. L. White	£26.05
Single	inc.	506	Mrs C. Syms	£40.14

List of transactions

0715	Early morning tea to all residents
0720	Telephone calls: Room 501 £1.06 Room 506 65p
0730	Disbursements: Room 504 razor blades 55p Room 506 dry cleaning £2.50
0830	Breakfast to all residents: 12 chance breakfasts
0900	Allowance and adjustments (correction of yesterday's tab): Room 501 omission of guests' lunch charge £4.25 Room 504 overcharge on yesterday's lunch 55p Room 503 charged £1.20 for taxi instead of room 506
0930	Departure: Room 501 Mr Williams pays by cheque less an amount of £55 received as an advance deposit
0945	Mrs Syms moves to room 509, a twin with bath, and is joined by her husband; terms fully inclusive
1000	Room 503 pays £25 on account
1030	Arrival: Mr and Mrs B. Downs given Room 501, terms R & B
1100	Morning coffee served to all residents, chance coffees £3.50
1130	Rev. White checks out, pays cash
1135	Arrival: Ms Payne given Room 510, single without bath, terms inclusive
1300	Lunches: Room 503 2 lunches, 1 coffee, wine £3.25, cigar 50p Room 501 2 lunches, 2 coffees Chance lunches £42.50, beverages £4.40, wine £24.10, cigarettes £3.20, spirits £5.10
1430	Change of room: Ms Payne moves to Room 504
1500	Arrival: Mr and Mrs O. Shaw given Room 507, twin without bath, terms inclusive, Mrs Shaw pays for three nights in advance
1700	Directors meeting of Mayo Ltd held in Court Room; room hire £30, 12 teas at 40p, 12 dinners at £6.25, private bar £28.75; account transferred to ledger folio 15
1800	Lounge bar pays in £204.25

A6.9 (a) Enter on the visitors' tabular ledger sheet the particulars of the guests listed below who are in residence when you come on duty in the morning.

(b) Enter all the transactions listed below in chronological order.

(c) Finally, close and balance the tab as if it were at the end of the day's business, adding and reconciling all totals.

Tariff of the Glanville Hotel

Room and breakfast	£18 (inc. of £2 breakfast per person)
Inclusive terms	£25 (£12 board per person)
Private bathroom	£5 per room per night
Early morning beverages	40p per person
Morning coffee	50p per person
Luncheon (table d'hôte)	£3.75 per person
Meal beverages	40p per person

Note:

Terms are charged in advance, and for new arrivals immediately upon
arrival. Inclusive terms cover room, breakfast, lunch, afternoon tea
and dinner only. All charges quoted are inclusive of service charge
and VAT.

List of guests in residence

Type	Terms	Name	Room no.	Balance b/f
Double with bath	R & B	Mr and Mrs V. Kettle	107	£46.44
Twin with bath	inc.	Mr and Mrs C. Potts	110	£52.90
Single with bath	R & B	Mr G. Denton	112	£22.22
Single	R & B	Ms J. Paige	121	£20.79

List of transactions

0730	Early morning beverages to all residents
	Newspapers:
	Room 107 40p
	Room 110 40p
	Room 112 20p
	Room 121 20p
	Telephone calls:
	Room 112 48p
	Room 121 £1.54
0845	Breakfast to all residents
0900	Chance breakfasts £12
0900	Departure: Room 107, Mr Kettle pays in cash less £25 received as an advance deposit
0915	Disbursements:
	Room 110 laundry £1.95
	Room 112 dry cleaning £2.50
	Room 121 medicine £1
0930	Allowances and adjustments for correction of errors on yesterday's tab:
	Room 110 omission of £2.10 taxi fare
	Room 121 overcharge of 65p for wine at lunch
0945	Mr Denton checks out settling his bill by cheque
1000	Room 121 Ms J. Paige departs settling her bill by cash
1000	Room 110 pays £20 cheque on account
1030	Arrival: Mr A. Turner given Room 112 on inclusive terms
1100	Morning coffee to all residents; chance morning coffees £3.50
1100	Arrival: Mr and Mrs B. Lydd given Room 107 on R & B terms
1300	Lunches:
	Room 107 2 lunches, beverages 80p, wine £2.30
	Room 112 1 lunch, beverage 40p, brandy 90p

Room 110 2 lunches, beverages 80p, wine £2.70

Chance lunches £22.50, beverages £3.20, spirits £4.70, wines £7.60, cigarettes £3.00, cigars £2.70

1430 Change of room: Mr Turner moves to Room 121

1445 Arrival: Miss O. Smith given Room 112, terms R & B; pays two nights in advance

1500 Carpet exhibition in Tower Room by Custom Carpets Ltd, room hire £60, buffet lunch for 22 people at £4.50 per person, private bar £41.50, flowers supplied by hotel £15; account transferred to ledger (folio 12)

1530 Lounge bar pays in £176.67 cash

7 Accounting for Wages

Calculating and paying wages is a task that has to be dealt with by every business, whether it has 50 or 500 employees, and the same routines are involved in each. These are:

1. Calculating the gross pay of every employee.
2. Calculating the deductions, such as income tax and national insurance contributions.
3. Calculating the net pay.
4. Keeping all the necessary records required by the government relating to income tax and national insurance contributions.
5. Keeping the individual pay record of each employee.
6. Preparing the payroll.
7. Preparing advice slips for employees.

7.1   WAGES SYSTEMS

There are many sophisticated mechanized and computerized methods of dealing with wages for large companies but, as the majority of hotels are fairly small, many companies producing business systems have devised simple wages systems to meet the needs of the small business.

It is impossible to illustrate all the systems on the market, but the Kalamazoo wages system illustrated is a typical example of how the operation has been simplified. Three records are involved:

1. The payroll sheet (Fig. 7.1).
2. The individual pay record (which replaces the government tax card P11) (Fig. 7.2).
3. The employee's pay advice slip (Fig. 7.3).

By using the special writing board provided (Fig. 7.4) and using special forms which are produced on IDEM paper (no carbon required), all records are written simultaneously. Each pay advice slip is folded only once and fits neatly into a window envelope so that only the employee's name is showing, thus making it unnecessary to write the name on the envelope.

The advantages of the system are:

1. Written work is reduced.
2. There is no copying between records, thus eliminating the chance of copying errors.
3. Employees receive an easily understood payslip.

Pay Roll

Week or Month No.	Date	1	9/4																				
Details																								
	A	60	—																					
Earnings	B	10	—																					
	C	5	—																					
	D																							
	E																							
	Gross Pay	75	—																					
Superannuation																								
Gross Pay for Tax Purposes		75	—																					
Gross Pay to Date for Tax Purposes		75	—																					
Tax Free Pay		24	80																					
Taxable Pay to Date		50	20																					
Tax Due to Date		17	50																					
Tax Refund																								
	Tax	17	50																					
	N.I. Contribution (Employee)	4	31																					
	0																							
	1																							
Deductions	2																							
	3																							
	4																							
	5																							
	6																							
	Total Deductions	21	81																					
Net Pay		53	19																					
F																								
G																								
Total Amount Payable		53	19																					
N.I. Contribution (Employer)																								
N.I. Total (Employer & Employee)		12	37																					
H																								
Contracted-out Contribution included above																					£20			
																					£10			
																					£5			
NAME		Miller																			£1			
																					50p			
																					10p			
		K.E.																			5p			
																					2p			
																					1p			

Figure 7.1 *Payroll sheet. Reproduced with the permission of Kalamazoo Business Systems.*

4. It provides an individual pay record as evidence of compliance with the Wages Councils Act 1979.
5. Important pay records are securely filed.
6. The system is fully approved by the Inland Revenue and is kept up to date with new legislation.

7.2 PAYE (PAY AS YOU EARN)

To operate the PAYE system the employer requires:

1. A deductions working sheet (P11) for each employee (or approved individual pay record).
2. A code number for each employee which reflects the tax allowances to which the employee is entitled.
3. Tax tables.
4. An end of year return (P14).

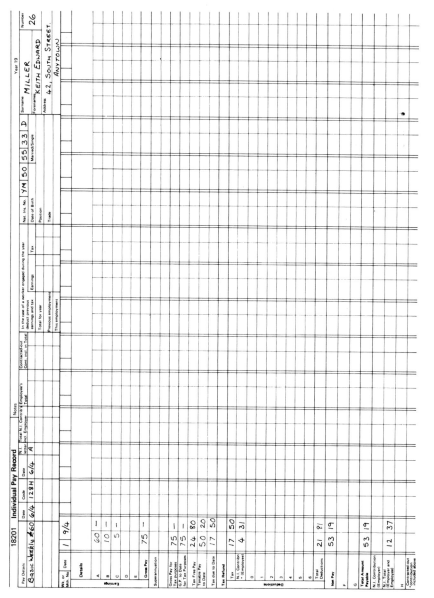

Figure 7.2   *Individual pay record. Reproduced with the permission of Kalamazoo Business Systems.*

PAY ADVICE

Week or Month no.	Date		9/4
Details			
Earnings A		60	—
B		10	—
C		5	—
D			
E			
Gross Pay		75	—
Superannuation			
Gross Pay for Tax Purposes		75	—
Gross Pay to Date for Tax Purposes		75	—
Tax Free Pay		24	80
Taxable Pay to Date		50	20
Tax Due to Date		17	50
Tax Refund			
Deductions Tax		17	50
* N.I. Contribution (Employee)		4	31
0			
1			
2			
3			
4			
5			
6			
Total Deductions		21	81
Net Pay		53	19
F			
G			
Total Amount Payable		53	19
N.I. Contribution (Employer)			
N.I. Total (Employer & Employee)		12	37
H			
* Contracted-out Contribution included above			

**YOUR PAY IS
MADE UP AS
SHOWN ABOVE**

Miller
K.E.

Figure 7.3 *Employee's pay advice slip. Reproduced with the permission of Kalamazoo Business Systems.*

Figure 7.4   *Copywriter board. Reproduced with the permission of Kalamazoo Business Systems.*

The amount of tax to be deducted is calculated in the following way:

1. The gross pay due to the employee is calculated and added to his or her previous payments made from 6 April (the beginning of each financial year).
2. Using the employee's code number and the free pay tables, the code number will indicate the proportion of the employee's allowances from 6 April to date and this amount is subtracted from the total pay to date. The balance left is the taxable pay to date.
3. The tax due is ascertained by looking up the taxable pay to date as shown by the taxable pay tables (tables B, C or D).
4. From the figure of the tax due to date the total tax paid already is deducted, leaving the tax to be deducted from the employee's pay for that week.
5. If the figure shown by the tax tables is less than the tax already deducted the employer must give the employee a refund of the difference.

Tax code numbers

An employee's code number may be any of the following:

1. A number followed by the suffix H, L, P, T or V, e.g. 193L. These code numbers are the normal codes to be used in conjunction with the free pay tables A and the taxable pay tables.

2. A code with the prefix D, e.g. D4. This relates to the higher rates of tax, for which tax tables D are used.
3. A code with the prefix F, used in conjunction with table F, the tax reckoner for prefix F codes.
4. Code BR. This code is to be used in conjunction with taxable pay table B.
5. Code NT, which stands for no tax. No tax is deducted but a record must be kept of the amount of pay, and the employer cannot refund any previous tax paid unless directed by the tax office.
6. Code OT, which stands for no free pay, means that no personal allowances are set against pay, so tax is deductible on the total pay by reference to taxable pay table B.

If an employee's circumstances change then the tax office will amend the code number.

Example 1

	£
Weekly earnings	200
Tax free pay (according to	
personal allowances code number)	120
Taxable pay	80

Tax tables and commonly used forms

The Inland Revenue will supply all tables and documents necessary for operating the PAYE system and will always give advice when difficulties arise. The most commonly used forms and documents are:

1. A set of tax tables consisting of: table A, free pay tables; tables B–D, taxable pay tables; and table F, tax reckoner for prefix F codes.
2. P7, an employer's guide to PAYE.
3. P6, Notice to employer of code number or amended code number.
4. P7x, instructions to employer, authority to amend suffix codes.
5. P8, blue card, instructions to employer on how to fill up deductions working sheet, on how to use tax tables and on how to make end of year return.
6. P9, notice to employer of changed code for the coming year.
7. P11, deductions working sheet for both weekly and monthly paid employees (Fig. 7.5).
8. P13, employer's permanent record of employees' details (Fig. 7.6).
9. P14, end of year return of pay, tax and national insurance contributions (Fig. 7.7).
10. P15, a coding claim form to be completed by new employees, e.g. school leavers and college leavers who have no code number.
11. P34, employer's requisition form.
12. P35, employer's annual statement, declaration and certificate.
13. P35x, notes for guidance on completion of form P35.
14. P38, an employer's supplementary return.
15. P38S, students employed during vacation, declaration by employer and statement by student.
16. P45. When an employee leaves a certificate P45 must be prepared in accordance with the direction on the form. Parts 2 and 3 are handed to the employee when leaving. Part 1 is sent to the local tax office. Parts 2 and 3 are handed by the employee to the new

Deductions working sheet P11 (New)	Employee's surname *(in BLOCK letters)*	First two forenames	Tax Code†	Amended code†				Year to 5 April 19......
Employer's name				Week/Month no. in which applied				
Tax District and reference	National Insurance no.	Date of birth *in figures* Day Month Year	Works no. etc.	Date of leaving *in figures* Day Month Year				

National Insurance Contributions*					PAYE Income Tax						
Total of Employee's and Employer's Contributions payable 1a	Employee's Contributions payable 1b	Employee's contributions at Contracted-out rate (included in column 1b) 1c	MONTH number	WEEK number	Pay in the week or month 2	Total pay to date 3	Total free pay to date as shown by Table A 4	Total taxable pay to date • 5	Total tax due to date as shown by Taxable Pay Tables 6	Tax deducted or refunded in the week or month *Mark refunds "R"* 7	For employer's use
£	£	£	6 April to 5 May	1	£	£	£	£	£	£	
				2							
				3							
			1	4							
			6 May to 5 June	5							
				6							
				7							
			2	8							
			6 June to 5 July	9							
				10							
				11							
				12							
			3	13							
			6 July to 5 Aug.	14							
				15							
				16							
			4	17							
			6 Aug. to 5 Sept.	18							
				19							
				20							
			5	21							
			6 Sept. to 5 Oct.	22							
				23							
				24							
				25							
			6	26							
			6 Oct. to 5 Nov.	27							
				28							
				29							
			7	30							
Total carried forward	Total carried forward	Total carried forward									

*N.I. Contribution Table letter must be entered overleaf beside the N.I. totals boxes - *see the note shown there.*

◀ This box may be used if the employer wishes to record the N.I. letter while this side of the sheet is in use.

† *If amended cross out previous code.*

• *If in any week/month the amount in column 4 is more than the amount in column 3, make no entry in column 5.*

P11 (New)

Figure 7.5 *Deductions working sheet, P11 (New). Reproduced with the permission of the Controller of Her Majesty's Stationery Office.*

PAYE: EMPLOYER'S PERMANENT RECORD OF EMPLOYEES

Name of employee	Payroll no. etc.	National Insurance number	Date of birth	Date started	Tax Office notification (P45(3) or P46)	Date P45 (3) or P46 sent to Tax Office	Date left	Date P45 (1) sent to Tax Office	Notes

P13 This form is for optional use by the employer.

Figure 7.6 *PAYE: Employer's permanent record of employees, P13. Reproduced with the permission of the Controller of Her Majesty's Stationery Office.*

End of Year Return P14 DHSS COPY

Employer's full name and address		Tax District and reference		Year to 5 April
		Works no. etc.		**19**

Employee's National Insurance number	Employee's date of birth *(in figures)* Day Month Year	Employee's surname *(in BLOCK CAPITALS)*	First two forenames	Final tax code

Total for year		Previous employment		This employment	Tax deducted or refunded *If refund mark "R"*	Date of leaving if before 5 April *(in figures)* Day Month Year
Pay	Tax deducted	Pay	Tax deducted	Pay		
£	£	£	£	£	£	

National Insurance contributions in this employment				Employee's Widows and Orphans/life insurance contributions in this employment	Holiday pay paid but not included in pay above	Payment in Week 53 *Include pay and tax in totals above and enter X, 54 or 56 in this box (see Employer's Guide)*	For official use
Contribution Table letter	Total of Employee's and Employer's Contributions payable 1a	Employee's Contributions payable 1b	Employee's Contributions at Contracted-out rate included in column 1b 1c				
	£	£	£				P9D/P11D
	£	£	£	£	£		
	£	£	£				
	£	£	£				

Please do not write in this space

DIRECTORS AND CERTAIN EMPLOYEES:
A return on form P11D or P11 D(a) is required.
OTHER EMPLOYEES:
A return on form P9D is required only where payments of the nature described on the form have been made.

P14

V.B.F. Ltd. 10/81 Dd. 8252369 52-3540/1A 910/55 40922

Figure 7.7 *End of year return, P14. Reproduced with the permission of the Controller of Her Majesty's Stationery Office.*

employer, who will prepare a deductions working sheet (P11) from the information on the P45. Part 3 is then completed, detached and sent to the new employer's local tax office (Fig. 7.8).

17. P46, particulars of an employee for whom no code number has been notified to the employer or who has not produced Parts 2 and 3 of a P45; this must be completed by the employer and sent to the tax office immediately.
18. P47, employer's application to the tax office for authority to refund tax over £50.
19. P48, authority from the tax office to refund income tax of over £50 to an employee.
20. P60, employer's certificate of pay and tax deductions, to be given to employees at the end of each year.

Commencement of the tax year 6 April

At the start of the tax year employers should prepare for each employee for whom a deductions working sheet was in use on 5 April, and who is still in their employment, a new deductions working sheet (P11) and enter:

1. The employee's surname and forenames.
2. The employee's national insurance number.
3. Date of birth (if known).
4. Name and reference number of PAYE tax office.
5. National insurance contribution table letter.

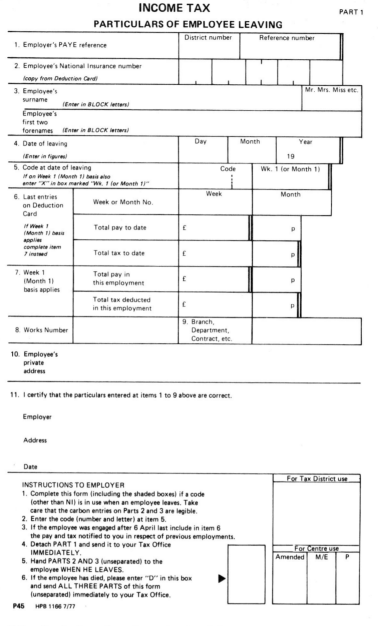

Figure 7.8   *Particulars of employee leaving, P45. Reproduced with the permission of the Controller of Her Majesty's Stationery Office.*

End of tax year returns

At the end of the tax year an end of year return form (P14) and a P60 must be completed for each employee for whom the employer has used a deductions working sheet during the year. This includes employees who left during the year. Completed returns will show:

1. Employer's name and address.
2. Employer's tax district and PAYE reference number.
3. Year to which the return refers.

4. Employee's national insurance number.
5. Employee's date of birth (if known).
6. Employee's surname and up to two forenames.
7. Final tax code number.
8. Total pay and tax deducted during the year.
9. Figures of national insurance contributions.

All returns must be completed and returned to the Collector of Taxes accompanied by the employer's annual statement and declaration certificate P35, which is a summary of all employees for whom a deductions working sheet was used during the tax year.

Approved business system

The Kalamazoo end of year tax returns system which is approved by the Inland Revenue, uses substitute forms (P11(S)) produced on carbonless paper so that pay and deductions are recorded on all forms simultaneously. The records are:

1. P11(S) in duplicate. Both copies are sent to the Inland Revenue; one copy they retain, the other they pass on to the Department of Health and Social Security.
2. P35, a substitute for the official P35 but produced on carbonless paper.
3. P60, a substitute for the official P60.

The P11(S) copies and P60 are produced as a three-part set.
   The system works in the following way:

1. At the end of the tax year the employer heads up a three-part set for each employee showing name, national insurance number, and so on.
2. The set is then placed over a P35 substitute on a special writing board which holds the forms in alignment (see Fig. 7.9).

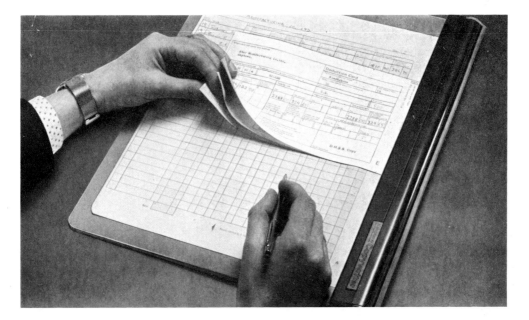

Figure 7.9   *End of year tax returns. Reproduced with the permission of Kalamazoo Business Systems.*

3. Details of the year's pay and deductions are entered on the top copy of the set, thus completing the figures on all four copies simultaneously.
4. Having completed a set for each employee the employer now has a full list of tax and national insurance deductions on the P35 substitute. The totals *only* are then transferred to the official P35 Part 1(b).
5. The returns are now ready to be submitted to the local tax office. The P60s are given to the employees and the two P11(S) copies, together with the P35 substitute and official P35 declaration and Part 1(b), are sent to the Inland Revenue.

Dealing with leavers

When employees leave the three-part set and the P35 are completed so that at the end of the year the job is already done and figures are included automatically in the returns.

Foreign employees

A person from abroad taking employment in the United Kingdom should have his or her pay subjected to the normal PAYE procedures.

Casual employees

PAYE should be operated if the employee's pay exceeds the PAYE threshold. If the employee's pay is less, a record must still be kept of the employee's name, address and wages earned.

Gratuities, service charge and tronc

Gratuities from customers or service charge paid out to employees should be included in the pay on the deductions working sheet. When sums are paid out of a tronc the troncmaster or troncmistress is responsible for the tax deductions under the PAYE system in respect of sums distributed to the members of the tronc. The troncmaster should enter the word 'tronc' in the space on the end of year returns.

Meal vouchers

Meal vouchers are not regarded as part of the taxable income provided that they satisfy certain conditions.

Accommodation and meals

The following items are not treated as 'pay' for tax deduction purposes:

1. Expenses incurred by employees in performance of their duties.
2. Rent-free accommodation because of the nature of employees' duties.
3. Free board or lodgings made available by the employer.

7.3   NATIONAL INSURANCE CONTRIBUTIONS

The Social Security Pension Act 1975 provides for retirement and widow's pensions to consist of two parts:

1. The basic pension.
2. An additional pension related to earnings.

Both parts will be paid for by national insurance contributions, but employers who are members of occupational pension schemes may be contracted out of the additional part of the retirement and widow's pension. In this case national insurance contributions will be reduced for both employees and employers.

Class I contributions

These contributions are earnings related and are payable as a percentage of earnings subject to specified upper and lower earnings limits. They are collected along with PAYE income tax and entered on the deductions working sheet P11 (new).

Married women

Married women under the age of 60 generally have to pay the standard-rate insurance contributions, but up to 5 April 1977 they were given the choice of electing for reduced liability, which means they pay reduced-rate contributions which do not count for benefit purposes.

National insurance numbers

The Department of Social Security allocates a national insurance number to every contributor and this number must be recorded on all employment records. Employees must give their NI number to their employers on request, and anyone who is unable to produce his or her NI number must apply to the local social security office or careers office if under the age of 18.

Contribution rates

These will vary from time to time depending on government legislation, but as an example the 1982 contributions were as shown in Table 7.1.

There are six main contribution tables, each bearing an identifying letter. These tables are contained in two volumes:

1. *Volume 1 (not contracted out)*
   Table A, standard rate contributions
   Table B, reduced rate contributions
   Table C, employer only contributions
2. *Volume 2 (contracted out)*
   Table D, standard rate contributions
   Table E, reduced rate contributions
   Table C, employer only contributions

Table 7.1   *1982 national insurance contribution rates*

Not contracted out	Employee		Employer	
standard rate	7.75%		13.7%	
reduced rate	2.75%		13.7%	
men over 65				
women over 60	nil		nil	
children under 16				
people earning under £29.50 per week	nil		nil	
Contracted out	On first £27	Earnings between £27 and £200	On first £27	Earnings between £27 and £200
standard rate	7.75%	5.25%	13.7%	9.2%
reduced rate	2.75%	2.75%	13.7%	9.2%
people earning under £29.50 per week	nil	–	nil	–

It is important that the correct table is used and that the table letter and totals of contributions paid under each table are entered on the deductions working sheet.

On the P14 end of year return it is important that the table letter and the correct total are transferred to the return.

7.4   WAGES COUNCILS

The Employment Protection Act 1975 extended the powers of the wages councils covering parts of the hotel and catering industry. They can now fix all terms and conditions of service and are no longer restricted to those affecting pay and holidays. There are five separate wages councils implementing the Wages Councils Act 1959, though these are likely to become amalgamated or changed in the future. At the time of writing they are:

1. The Industrial and Staff Canteen Undertaking Wages Council (ISC).
2. The Unlicensed Place of Refreshment Wages Council (UPR).
3. The Licensed Residential and Licensed Restaurant Wages Council (LR).
4. The Licensed Non-Residential Establishment Wages Council (LNR).
5. The Unlicensed Residential Establishment Wages Council (UR).

Wages council inspectors have the power to inspect records, to interview workers and to prosecute employers who do not observe all the statutory requirements. Schedules from the office of wages councils with all the orders and updated legislation are available to all employers, and all inquiries about minimum pay, holidays and holiday pay should be addressed to the senior wages inspectors of the Department of Employment.

7.5   THE PAYROLL

Three records are usually involved in paying wages or salaries: the payroll, the employee's individual record and a pay advice slip for the employee. As the information required in each case is almost identical, modern systems, by using IDEM paper, complete the three records simultaneously.

7.6 CASH ANALYSIS AND SUMMARY

When preparing wages for the pay envelopes of employees it is important that the cash ordered from the bank is in the exact denominations required for each individual envelope.

Example 2

The cash analysis and cash summary for the bank for the following payroll would be as shown below.

			Cash Analysis								
Payroll no.	Name	Net Pay £	£10	£5	£1	50p	20p	10p	5p	2p	1p
1	M. James	82.25	8		2		1		1		
2	O. Smith	62.20	6		2		1				
3	A. Sales	55.78	5	1		1	1		1	1	1
4	M. Horton	72.66	7		2	1		1	1		1
5	M. Carter	47.17	4	1	2			1	1	1	
6	K. Holmes	86.90	8	1	1	1	2				
7	S. Pitt	57.44	5	1	2		2			2	
8	J. Paige	44.57	4		4	1			1	1	
9	T. Peacock	77.48	7	1	2		2		1	1	1
10	C. Potts	66.30	6	1	1		1	1			
Totals		652.75	60	6	18	4	10	3	6	6	3

Cash Summary

		£
60 x £10	=	600.00
6 x £5	=	30.00
18 x £1	=	18.00
4 x 50p	=	2.00
10 x 20p	=	2.00
3 x 10p	=	0.30
6 x 5p	=	0.30
6 x 2p	=	0.12
3 x 1p	=	0.03
		652.75

7.7 COMPUTERIZED WAGES SYSTEM

In the age of technology and computerization many systems have been designed to the Inland Revenue specifications for the computerized payroll. The programs (software), which are used in conjunction with compatible computers (hardware), present few problems for those who have no previous computer experience. The main information that can be fed into the computers is as follows:

1. All tax codes, including all normal codes with suffix H, L, P, T or V, and also BR, D, F and week 1 Basis.
2. All NI codes: A, B, C, D and E.
3. Hourly, weekly and monthly paid staff.
4. Overtime rates.
5. Pre-tax adjustments.

  6. After-tax adjustments.
  7. Employees' data.
  8. Analysis of pay run.
  9. P35. At the end of the year all grand totals can be produced.
10. Print-outs. A very comprehensive pay slip is produced for the employee side by side with the employer's copies retained in a continuous strip for convenience.
11. Many other features if required.

ASSIGNMENTS

A7.1 Write notes on the purpose and use of the following income tax documents:

(a) P9   (f) P35
(b) P11   (g) P45
(c) P13   (h) P46
(d) P14   (i) P47
(e) P15   (j) P60

A7.2 A set of tax tables consists of tables A, tables B to D and tables F. To what do these tables refer?

A7.3 What is the income tax position with regard to the following:

(a) foreign employees;
(b) casual employees;
(c) gratuities;
(d) service charge;
(e) tronc;
(f) meal vouchers;
(g) accommodation and meals to employees?

A7.4 Explain the importance of an employee's national insurance number.

A7.5 What do you understand by the following:

(a) class I contributions;
(b) standard rate;
(c) reduced rate;
(d) not contracted out rates;
(e) contracted out rates?

A7.6 There are six main national insurance contribution tables. List them with their identifying letters.

A7.7 Name the five wages councils covering parts of the hotel and catering industry.

A7.8 Prepare a cash analysis and summary for the following payroll sheet:

Payroll no.	Name	Net pay
		£
1	A. Sparrow	96.35
2	B. Hawke	88.82
3	C. Eagle	77.63
4	D. Wren	49.97
5	E. Snipe	53.48
6	F. Jay	91.77
7	G. Swift	68.87
8	H. Robin	58.88
9	I. Swallow	37.26
10	J. Lark	46.69
Total		

A7.9   Describe a modern approved system of recording wages for smaller business, mentioning its advantages.

A7.10   At the end of every tax year employers have to comply with certain regulations regarding returns. What are these regulations?

A7.11   What are the advantages and disadvantages of a computerized payroll?

8 The Trial Balance

As the name implies, the trial balance is a list of balances extracted from the ledger accounts at the end of an accounting period. It is not part of the records but is prepared to check the arithmetical accuracy of the posting from the various journals to accounts in the ledger. Every account in the ledger with a balance is listed in the trial balance, the debit balances in one list and the credit balances in another. It provides a stepping-stone to the ultimate object of keeping the records – the preparation of the trading account, the profit and loss account and the balance sheet.

The following illustrate the accounts after they have been balanced at the end of the month.

Dr.   Capital (A/C no. 1)   Cr.

Date	Details	F	£	p	Date	Details	F	£	p
19_ _					19_ _ Jan. 1	Balance	b/d	100 000	00

Dr.   Cash (A/C no. 2)   Cr.

Date	Details	F	£	p	Date	Details	F	£	p
19_ _ Jan. 1	Balance	b/d	19 530	00					

Dr.   Leasehold Premises (A/C no. 3)   Cr.

Date	Details	F	£	p	Date	Details	F	£	p
19_ _ Jan. 1	Balance	b/d	90 000	00					

Dr.   Kitchen Equipment (A/C no. 4)   Cr.

Date	Details	F	£	p	Date	Details	F	£	p
19_ _ Jan. 1	Balance	b/d	12 400	00					

Dr.   China, Plate and Glass (A/C no. 5)   Cr.

Date	Details	F	£	p	Date	Details	F	£	p
19_ _ Jan. 1	Balance	b/d	2300	00					

Dr.   Fixtures and Fittings (A/C no. 6)   Cr.

Date	Details	F	£	p	Date	Details	F	£	p
19_ _ Jan. 1	Balance	b/d	9000	00					

Dr.   Stock (A/C no. 7)   Cr.

Date	Details	F	£	p	Date	Details	F	£	p
19_ _ Jan. 1	Balance	b/d	2000	00					

Dr.   Wages (A/C no. 8)   Cr.

Date	Details	F	£	p	Date	Details	F	£	p
19_ _ Jan. 1	Balance	b/d	32 000	00					

Dr.   Postage and Stationery (A/C no. 9)   Cr.

Date	Details	F	£	p	Date	Details	F	£	p
19_ _ Jan 1.	Balance	b/d	860	00					

Dr.   Gas and Electricity (A/C no. 10)   Cr.

Date	Details	F	£	p	Date	F	£	p
19_ _ Jan. 1	Balance	b/d	6300	00				

Dr.   Miscellaneous Expenses (A/C no. 11)   Cr.

Date	Details	F	£	p	Date	Details	F	£	p
19_ _ Jan. 1	Balance	b/d	700	00					

Dr.   Purchases (A/C no. 12)   Cr.

Date	Details	F	£	p	Date	Details	F	£	p
19_ _ Jan. 1	Balance	b/d	68 000	00					

Dr.   Purchases Returns (A/C no. 13)   Cr.

Date	Details	F	£	p	Date	Details	F	£	p
					19_ _ Jan. 1	Balance	b/d	450	00

Dr.   Sales (A/C no. 14)   Cr.

Date	Details	F	£	p	Date	Details	F	£	p
					19_ _ Jan. 1	Balance	b/d	140 200	00

Dr.   Bought Ledger Control (A/C no. 15)   Cr.

Date	Details	F	£	p	Date	Details	F	£	p
					19_ _ Jan. 1	Balance	b/d	3280	00

Dr.   Sales Ledger Control (A/C no. 16)   Cr.

Date	Details	F	£	p	Date	Details	F	£	p
19_ _ Jan. 1	Balance	b/d	840	00					

Trial Balance as at _ _

	Dr. £	Cr. £
Capital account		100 000
Cash account	19 530	
Leasehold premises	90 000	
Kitchen equipment	12 400	
China, plate and glass	2 300	
Fixtures and fittings	9 000	
Stock	2 000	
Wages	32 000	
Postage and stationery	860	
Gas and electricity	6 300	
Miscellaneous expenses	700	
Purchases	68 000	
Purchases returns		450
Sales		140 200
Purchases ledger control (creditors)		3 280
Sales ledger control (debtors)	840	
	243 930	243 930

Stock at end £1500

8.1 ERRORS REVEALED BY THE TRIAL BALANCE

When the ledger balances are listed and the total debits do not agree with the total credits, the discrepancy could be due to any of the following reasons: incorrect balance of the cash book; incorrect totals in purchases, purchases returns, allowances or sales daybooks; an entry posted to the wrong side of an account; an omission of a debit or credit in posting from the journals to the ledger; an incorrect figure posted from a journal to the ledger account; or discounts transferred incorrectly.

Incorrect balance of the cash book

Usually at the end of the month the cash payments book and the cash receipts book are totalled and the balances carried down to commence the next month's trading. If there is an arithmetical error in either of the totals or the balance carried down then the figure transferred will be incorrect and the trial balance will not agree. It is usual, however, to agree the cash balance with a physical cash count, and to check the bank balance by means of a bank reconciliation statement.

Incorrect totals in purchases, purchases returns, allowances or sales daybooks

Usually at the end of the month the totals of the subsidiary journals are transferred to the ledger. If there has been an arithmetical error in any of those totals it will be reflected in the figures transferred to the trial balance and the trial balance totals will not agree. However, if purchases and sales control accounts have been prepared errors should be highlighted before the trial balance takes place.

Entries posted to the wrong side of an account

If a cheque for £60 is received from Mr Jones and entered on the debit side of the cash book, then in error is posted to the debit side of Mr Jones's account instead of to the credit side, when Mr Jones's account is balanced an incorrect balance will be transferred to the trial balance and the totals of the trial balance will not agree.

Omission of a debit or a credit in posting from the journals to the ledger

If a cheque for £200 is paid out for insurance and entered into the cash payments book on the credit side, and then is not posted from the cash book to the debit side of the insurance account, an incorrect balance will be transferred to the trial balance and the totals of the trial balance will not agree.

Incorrect figures posted from a journal to the ledger account

An invoice for goods valued at £220 from L. Smith is entered in the purchases daybook, but the figure posted to L. Smith's account in the ledger is £200. When the balance of that account is transferred to the trial balance it will be incorrect and therefore the totals of the trial balance will not agree.

Discounts transferred incorrectly

Discounts allowed are entered on the debit side of the cash book and should be transferred in total to the debit side of the discounts allowed account in the ledger. Discounts received are entered on the credit side of the cash book and should be transferred in total to the credit side of the discounts received account in the ledger. If either of these is posted to the wrong side in the ledger account then the balances transferred to the trial balance will be incorrect and the trial balance will not agree.

8.2   PROCEDURES FOR LOCATING ERRORS IN THE TRIAL BALANCE

In a practical situation it would be normal procedure to:

1. Check the cash balance in the cash book against the actual cash in hand.
2. Check and reconcile the bank balance in the cash book against the balance in the bank statement.
3. Prove the sales and allowances figures against the tabular ledger and sales ledger control account.
4. Prove the purchases and purchases returns figures against the purchases control account.

If the totals of the trial balance still cannot be brought into agreement then the following step-by-step procedure should be adopted:

1. Check the addition of the totals in the trial balance, first adding top to bottom, then bottom to top.

2. Make sure that every ledger account with a balance has been included in the trial balance. Common omissions are cash, bank and discounts.
3. Find the difference between the trial balance totals. Halve the difference and look for any balance of this amount which may have been posted to the wrong side.
4. Check all the totals of the books of first entry, i.e. purchases, purchases returns, sales and sales allowances.
5. Check the balances of the ledger accounts for arithmetical accuracy.
6. Check all folio columns for any omissions in posting.
7. If the error is still elusive every item in the ledger accounts will have to be checked, ticking each amount both in the books of first entry and in the ledger accounts, looking for slides, e.g. £23.69 written as £32.69. Check to see if the difference is divisible by 9; if so it may indicate a reversal or slide of two figures, e.g. 23 as 32 (difference of 9), or 81 as 18 (difference of 63 = 7 x 9).

8.3   ERRORS NOT REVEALED BY THE TRIAL BALANCE

The agreement of the trial balance totals is not a guarantee that all transactions have been posted accurately to the ledger accounts. There are certain types of errors which a trial balance will not reveal; these are the most difficult errors to locate and only concentration and efficiency will help to eliminate them. They are errors of omission, errors of original entry, errors of principle, errors of commission, compensating errors and errors of duplication.

Errors of omission

This type of error occurs when an accounting document, e.g. an invoice or a credit note, is lost or mislaid, the result being that there is no debit or credit entry in either the book of first entry or the ledger account. In fact the transaction has been omitted completely from the accounts system, and consequently it will have no effect on the totals of the trial balance.

Errors of original entry

This type of error occurs when an amount on an invoice, e.g. £60, is entered wrongly in the book of first entry, e.g. as £66, and then is posted wrongly to the ledger account, e.g. as £66. As there has been a debit entry and a credit entry for the same amount, the totals of the trial balance will still be in agreement.

Errors of principle

This type of error occurs when a transaction has a debit entry and a credit entry but the item is posted in principle to the wrong classification of account, e.g. if a purchase invoice for fixtures and fittings is entered in the purchases daybook instead of the journal and the value included incorrectly in the total of purchases for resale in the ledger account. As there has been a debit entry and a credit entry for the same amount, the totals of the trial balance could still be in agreement.

Errors of commission

An example of this type of error is when a cheque has been received from R. Paige and has been debited correctly in the cash book, but when posted to the ledger it is credited to R. Paige's account. As there has been a debit entry and a corresponding credit entry for the same amount (although posted incorrectly to the wrong account), the totals of the trial balance could still be in agreement.

Compensating errors

An example of this type of error is where the wages account has been over-added by £20 and by coincidence the sales account has been over-added by £20, so an error of £20 on the debit side is compensated by an error of £20 on the credit side of the trial balance and the totals could still agree.

Errors of duplication

An example of this type of error is when the same invoice is entered into the purchases day-book twice and posted from there to the ledger account twice. The totals of the trial balance could still be in agreement, as there have been two debit entries and two corresponding credit entries.

8.4   THE SUSPENSE ACCOUNT

At the end of a trading period, when a trial balance is extracted from the ledger and the totals do not agree, the step-by-step procedure should be followed in order to locate the errors causing the disagreement. However, this can sometimes be a long, tedious task and it would not be sensible to spend a long time searching for small amounts in order to balance the trial balance. Therefore a suspense account is created in the ledger and either debited or credited with the difference in the trial balance. When the errors are revealed a journal entry is made to correct the errors and the amounts involved are transferred from the suspense account, thus eliminating any balance.

Example

On 31 December a trial balance extracted from the books of the James Hotel showed that the credit side total was greater than the debit side total by £450. As the amount was small in comparison with the totals of the trial balance, after a summary search for the errors the amount was transferred to a suspense account in the ledger.

Dr.   Suspense A/C   Cr.

Date	Details	F	£	p	Date	Details	F	£	p
19_ _ Dec. 31	Difference in trial balance		450	00					

During the month of January the following errors were revealed:

1. The sales daybook had been overcast by £200.
2. A cheque received from Jones Bros for £75 had been debited in the cash book but not credited to their account.
3. A cheque for £300 paid for insurance had been credited in the cash book but not debited to the insurance account.
4. The purchases account had been undercast by £25 in December.

The journal entries to correct these errors and the suspense and ledger accounts are shown below.

General Journal

Date		Details	F	Dr.	Cr.
19_ _ Dec.	31	Suspense A/C		£ p 450.00	£ p
		difference in trial balance			450.00
Jan.	31	Sales A/C		200.00	
		Suspense A/C			200.00
		Being correction of December sales overcast by £200			
	31	Suspense A/C		75.00	
		Jones Bros A/C			75.00
		Being cheque received but not posted from cash book to customer's A/C			
	31	Insurance A/C		300.00	
		Suspense A/C			300.00
		Being cheque paid but not posted to insurance A/C			
	31	Purchases A/C		25.00	
		Suspense A/C			25.00
		Being purchases A/C undercast by £25 in December			

Suspense A/C

Dr. Date	Details	F	£	p	Cr. Date	Details	F	£	p
19_ _ Jan. 1	Balance (Difference in trial balance)		450	00	19_ _ Jan. 31	Sales A/C		200	00
					31	Insurance A/C		300	00
					31	Purchases A/C		25	00
31	Jones Bros.		75	00					
			525	00				525	00

Sales A/C

Dr. Date	Details	F	£	p	Cr. Date	Details	F	£	p
19_ _ Jan. 31	Suspense A/C		200	00					

Jones Bros A/C

Dr. Date	Details	F	£	p	Cr. Date	Details	F	£	p
					19_ _ Jan. 31	Suspense A/C		75	00

Dr.   Insurance A/C   Cr.

Date	Details	F	£	p	Date	Details	F	£	p
19_ _ Jan. 31	Suspense A/C		300	00					

Dr.   Purchases A/C   Cr.

Date	Details	F	£	p	Date	Details	F	£	p
19_ _ Jan. 31	Suspense A/C		25	00					

ASSIGNMENTS

A8.1   Explain the purpose of the trial balance and its limitations.

A8.2   Give examples of the types of errors which could be responsible for disagreement between the total debit balances and the total credit balances in the trial balance.

A8.3   What steps would you take to locate errors if the totals of the trial balance did not agree?

A8.4   Explain what is meant, giving examples in each case, by the following types of errors in book-keeping:
(a) an error of omission;
(b) an error of commission;
(c) an error of principle;
(d) an error of original entry;
(e) a compensating error;
(f) an error of duplication.

A8.5   Explain the purpose and function of the suspense account.

A8.6   The following list of balances was extracted from the accounts of the Southward Hotel. Prepare a trial balance as at 31 December 19＿＿.

	£
Capital	125 000
Cash in hand	280
Cash at bank	32 000
Sales	120 300
Purchases	41 500
Sales allowances	110
Purchases returns	450
Sundry debtors	1 100
Sundry creditors	2 580
Kitchen equipment	7 500
Restaurant furniture	10 000
China, plate and glass	1 500
Gas, electricity, fuel	3 200
Repairs and renewals	1 750
Sundry expenses	1 900
Freehold premises	105 000
Stock 1 January	1 900
Wages and salaries	40 590
Stock 31 December 19＿＿	1 200

After agreeing the trial balance prepare a trading account, profit and loss account and balance sheet, as illustrated in Chapter 2, The Ledger.

A8.7   From the following list of balances extracted from the accounts of the Northward Hotel prepare a trial balance as at 31 December 19_ _ .

	£
Sales	155 000
Purchases	49 500
Sales allowances	350
Returns out	610
Leasehold premises	80 000
Fixtures and fittings	15 000
Equipment	8 000
Rent and rates	7 200
Gas and electricity	5 000
Wages and salaries	55 600
Insurance	1 550
Advertising	1 380
Repairs and renewals	3 200
Stock 1 January	800
Cash in hand	400
Bank overdraft	10 000
Loan from M. James	5 000
Sundry debtors	200
Sundry creditors	2 800
Laundry	750
Discount allowed	210
Discount received	155
Drawings	6 000
Capital	61 575
Stock 31 December 19_ _	950

After agreeing the trial balance prepare a trading account, profit and loss account and balance sheet as illustrated in Chapter 2, The Ledger.

A8.8 The following exercise contains errors. Correct the errors and agree the trial balance as at 30 June 19_ _.

	Dr. £	Cr. £
Capital		49 800
Stock 1 July	600	
Loan from O. Smith	10 000	
Sales	80 500	
Purchases		30 400
Leasehold premises	50 000	
Kitchen equipment	6 000	
Restaurant furniture	10 000	
China, plate and glass	3 000	
Linen	500	
Debtors		200
Creditors	1 620	
Rent and rates	5 000	
Wages and salaries	25 200	
Advertising	800	
Maintenance repairs	1 100	
Insurance		800
Telephone	1 300	
Printing and stationery	570	
Sundry expenses		1 900
Cash in hand	2 400	
Sales allowances		150
Gas and electricity	2 000	
	200 590	83 250

Stock 30 June 19_ _ £430

After agreeing the trial balance prepare a trading account, profit and loss account and balance sheet as at 30 June 19_ _, as illustrated in Chapter 2, The Ledger.

A8.9   Correct and agree the following trial balance as at 31 March 19__ and then prepare the trading account, profit and loss account and balance sheet as illustrated in Chapter 2, The Ledger.

	Dr.	Cr.
	£	£
Capital		139 140
Fixtures and fittings	1 500	
Restaurant furniture	5 000	
Kitchen equipment	8 500	
China, plate, glass and linen	3 500	
Laundry		710
Printing and stationery	2 400	
Postage and telephone	1 520	
Purchases	46 170	
Sales		110 300
Maintenance		1 750
Advertising	4 300	
Debtors	1 200	
Creditors		4 870
Bank overdraft	12 000	
Wages and salaries	28 800	
Rates		3 700
Freehold premises	143 000	
Stock 1 April		2 100
Discount received	290	
Fuel and light	4 700	
Cash in hand	2 250	
Sundry expenses	2 000	
Repairs and renewals	3 500	
	270 630	262 570

Stock 31 March £1600

A8.10   On 31 March 19__ the trial balance extracted from the ledger of the books of the Murray Hotel showed that the credit side total was greater by £620 than the debit side total. To save time it was decided to transfer the difference to a suspense account. During the course of the month of April the following errors were disclosed. Show the journal entries and the suspense and ledger account entries necessary to correct the errors and eliminate any suspense account balance.

Apr. 30   The purchases returns account had been overcast by £34.

30   The discount allowed total £36 had not been posted from the cash book to the ledger account.

30   A cheque for £50 received from R. White had been entered in the cash book but not posted to R. White's ledger account.

30   The cash book debit balance had been carried down as £6000 instead of £6600.

A8.11 On 31 December 19–– the trial balance extracted from the ledger of the books of the Queen's Hotel showed that the total of the debit side was greater by £840 than the total of the credit side. After summary search failed to locate the errors causing the disagreement, the £840 was transferred to a suspense account. During the preparation of the trial balance on 31 January the following errors were revealed:

(a) The debit balance of the advertising account in the ledger had been undercast by £200.

(b) Cash sales of £400 had been debited in the cash book but not posted to the sales account in the ledger.

(c) A cheque for £640 received from M. Horton had been debited in the cash book but not posted to M. Horton's account in the ledger.

(d) £100 cash credited in the cash payments book for provisions had not been posted to the purchases account in the ledger.

Show the journal and ledger entries to correct the errors and illustrate the suspense account after the corrections have been made, bringing down any balance that remains as at 31 January 19––.

9 The Final Accounts

9.1 TRIAL BALANCE AND FINAL ACCOUNTS

As we saw in Chapter 8, the trial balance is a list of all the debit and credit balances extracted from the accounts in the ledger at a given date. It is a method of checking the arithmetical accuracy of the posting from the subsidiary books to the ledger accounts. Once the trial balance has been agreed as correct it can be used for the preparation of the final accounts, i.e.

1. The trading account, in which the gross profit for the trading period under review is ascertained.
2. The profit and loss account, in which the net profit for the period is ascertained.
3. The balance sheet, which is a list of the assets and liabilities of the business at a given date.

9.2 TERMS AND DEFINITIONS USED IN THE STANDARD SYSTEM OF HOTEL ACCOUNTS

Certain terms and definitions are used in book-keeping, and these should be clearly understood so that the balance of each account is transferred under its correct heading in the final accounts. The hotel and catering industry is specialized and the types of purchases, sales and expenses are relevant only to hotel and catering establishments. Therefore the names of the accounts found in the trading and the profit and loss accounts and the balance sheet are directly related to the hotel and catering industry, as shown below.

Trading account

Sales	*Purchases*	*Stock*
Guest accommodation	Food purchases	Food
Restaurants	Liquor purchases	Liquor
Bars	Tobacco purchases	Tobacco
Banquets	Cost of staff meals and liquor (Cr.)	
Services to guests (on tabular ledger)		

Profit and loss account

Expenses	*Income received which is added to gross profit*
Kitchen fuel	Rents received
Heating fuel	Commission received
Repairs and renewals	Profit on currency exchange
Gas	Discounts received
Electricity	
Water rates	
Telephone	
Postage	
Cleaning supplies	
Credit card charges	
Insurances	
Licences	
Travelling expenses	
Professional fees	
Rates	
Loan interest	
Bank overdraft interest	
Depreciation	
Sundry expenses	
Commissions payable	
Wages and salaries	
Sundry expenses	

Balance sheet

Fixed assets

These are assets that are of a fixed nature and not intended for resale to customers, but used in the running of the business. For example:

Freehold premises
Leasehold premises
Kitchen equipment
Restaurant furniture
Fixtures and fittings
China, plate, glass, linen and cutlery
Office equipment
Office furniture

Current assets

These assets, as the name implies, are continually changing in value. For example:

Cash in hand
Cash in the bank

Stocks of food, drink and tobacco
Debtors
Prepayments of expenses or expenses in advance

Capital

This is the excess of assets over liabilities and is a liability in that it represents what the business owes to the owners.

Working capital

This represents the excess of current assets over current liabilities. CA – CL = WC (working capital).

Long-term liabilities

These are liabilities of a more permanent nature extending over a period of time. For example:

Mortgages
Bank loans
Loans from other sources

Current liabilities

These liabilities, as the name implies, are continually changing in value. For example:

Bank overdrafts
Creditors
Amounts owing and unpaid
Advance deposits

9.3   STAFF MEALS

In the hotel and catering industry the majority of the establishments regard staff meals as a labour cost and the cost of staff meals is either credited to the purchases account and debited to a staff meals account in the ledger, or adjusted in the trading account, where staff meals are shown as deducted from the purchases for resale. In both cases the cost is shown in the profit and loss account (see section 9.4) as an expense.

Trading Account
for year ending 31 December 19_ _

Dr.	£	£		Cr.	£
Stock 1 January		2 750	Sales		157 316
Add purchases	63 950				
Less staff meals	3 950	60 000			
		62 750			
Less stock 31 December		2 970			
		59 780			
Gross profit		97 536			
		157 316			157 316

9.4 BALANCE DAY ADJUSTMENTS

The final accounts of a business should present as accurate an account as possible of the trading results under review so that reliable comparisons can be made with previous trading periods. Therefore on balancing day certain adjustments will need to be made so that all expenses incurred during that particular trading period are charged to that period whether they have been paid or not.

Example

The following trial balance had been extracted from the accounts of the Truro Hotel at 31 December 19_ _. The trading account (see section 9.3) had been prepared and adjustments had to be made in order to prepare the profit and loss account.

Trial Balance
as at 31 December 19_ _

	Dr. £	Cr. £
Capital		120 000
Stock 1 January	2 750	
Net purchases	60 000	
Sales		157 316
Wages	40 100	
Staff meals	3 950	
Printing and stationery	3 145	
Gas and electricity	6 300	
Postage and telephone	1 575	
Cash in bank	4 500	
Cash in hand	500	
Insurance	900	
Sundry expenses	1 500	
Kitchen equipment	8 000	
Fixtures and fittings	15 000	
China, plate and cutlery	5 000	
Freehold premises	125 000	
Creditors		904
	278 220	278 220

Stock at 31 December £2970

Adjustments
Wages owing £850
Insurance paid in advance £250

To make the adjustments:

1. Wages owing are added to the wages and salaries figure in the trial balance (£40 100 + £850 = £40 950) and this figure is debited in the profit and loss account, and the wages owing are shown as a current liability in the balance sheet.
2. Insurance prepaid is deducted from the insurance figure in the trial balance (£900 – £250 = £650) and this figure is debited in the profit and loss account, and the amount of the insurance prepaid is shown as a current asset in the balance sheet.

Profit and Loss Account
Dr.   for the year ending 31 December 19__   Cr.

	£	£		£
Wages and salaries	40 100		Gross profit	97 536
Add wages owing	850	40 950		
Staff meals		3 950		
Gas and electricity		6 300		
Printing and stationery		3 145		
Postage and telephone		1 575		
Insurance	900			
Less insurance prepaid	250	650		
Sundry expenses		1 500		
		58 070		
Net profit		39 466		
		97 536		97 536

Balance Sheet
Dr.   as at 31 December 19__   Cr.

	£	£		£	£
Capital	120 000		Fixed assets		
Add net profit	39 466	159 466	Freehold premises	125 000	
			Kitchen equipment	8 000	
			Fixtures and fittings	15 000	
			China, plate and		
			cutlery	5 000	153 000
Current liabilities			Current assets		
Creditors	904		Stock 31 December	2 970	
Wages owing	850	1 754	Cash	500	
			Bank	4 500	
			Insurance prepaid	250	8 220
		161 220			161 220

The wages and insurance ledger accounts would show the adjustments as follows.

Dr.   Wages Account   Cr.

Date	Details	F	£	p	Date	Details	F	£	p
19__	Total wages	CB	40 100	00	19__	Profit and Loss A/C		40 950	00
Dec. 31	Wages owing	c/d	850	00	Dec. 31				
31			40 950	00				40 950	00
					19__				
					Jan. 1	Wages owing		850	00

Dr.   Insurance Account   Cr.

Date	Details	F	£	p	Date	Details	F	£	p
19__					19__				
Dec. 31	Total insurance	CB	900	00	Dec. 31	Insurance prepaid	c/d	250	00
					31	Profit and loss A/C		650	00
			900	00				900	00
19__									
Jan. 1	Insurance prepaid	b/d	250	00					

9.5   BAD DEBTS

When all efforts have failed to recover money owing by a debtor to the business this is considered as a bad debt and the debtors account should be closed and the amount transferred to a bad debts account in the ledger. At balancing time bad debts are transferred to the profit and loss account as an expense.

Example

The following debit balances appeared in the accounts of the Bath Hotel:

	£
A. Tap	25.00
H. Waters	65.00
C. Plug	35.00

All efforts had failed to recover these debts so the following journal and ledger entries were made and the total of the bad debts account was debited to the profit and loss account as an expense on balancing day.

Journal   J1

Date	Details	Folio	Debit £	Credit £
19_ _ Dec. 31	Bad debts account A. Tap H. Waters C. Plug Being the transfer of irrecoverable bad debts to bad debts A/C	L10 L7 L8 L9	125.00	 25.00 65.00 35.00

Dr.   A. Tap (A/C no. 7)   Cr.

Date	Details	F	£	p	Date	Details	F	£	p
19_ _ Dec. 31	Balance	b/d	25	00	19_ _ Dec. 31	Transfer to bad debts	J1	25	00

Dr.   H. Waters (A/C no. 8)   Cr.

Date	Details	F	£	p	Date	Details	F	£	p
19_ _ Dec. 31	Balance	b/d	65	00	19_ _ Dec. 31	Transfer to bad debts	J1	65	00

Dr.   C. Plug (A/C no. 9)   Cr.

Date	Details	F	£	p	Date	Details	F	£	p
19_ _ Dec. 31	Balance	b/d	35	00	19_ _ Dec. 31	Transfer to bad debts	J1	35	00

Dr.   Bad Debts (A/C no. 10)   Cr.

Date	Details	F	£	p	Date	Details	F	£	p
19_ _ Dec. 31	Bad debts transferred	J1	125	00	19_ _ Dec. 31	To profit and loss A/C		125	00

Profit and Loss Account, 31 December 19_ _

Dr.   £   p   Cr.

	£	p		F	
Bad debts etc.	125	00	Gross profit	b/d	

9.6   DEPRECIATION

Depreciation is the loss in value of a fixed asset due to any of the following reasons:

1. Wear and tear. Kitchen equipment, fixtures and fittings, china, plate, cutlery, restaurant furniture, etc., will depreciate in value through continuous use.
2. Obsolescence. Any equipment that can be outdated by more modern equipment or change in fashion can lose value because of obsolescence, e.g. typewriters, certain kitchen equipment, etc.
3. Effluxion of time. The value of a lease of a premises will depreciate as time runs out. For example, if £10 000 were paid for a lease of premises for twenty years, in ten years that lease would be worth only £5000, for it would have lost value by the effluxion of time.

Depreciation is considered an expense and loss to the business, so at balancing time the depreciation of fixed assets is calculated and the value of the assets is reduced by the amount of depreciation. This amount is then debited in the profit and loss account as an expense to be set against the gross profit.

Methods of calculating depreciation

Straight line method

The value of the asset is divided by the number of years of life expectancy of the asset and a fixed sum is written off each year. For example, for a lease for twenty years valued at £10 000, the depreciation to be written off each year would be $\frac{£10\ 000}{20} = £500.$

Diminishing balance method

A fixed percentage, e.g. 10 per cent, is written off the balance every year. For example kitchen equipment purchased for £5000 is depreciated at 10 per cent each year. Therefore:

First year	£5000	– 10 per cent
Depreciation	500	
Second year	4500	– 10 per cent
Depreciation	450	
Third year	4050	and so on

Revaluation method

This method is used when obsolescence or change in fashion occurs, e.g. when an old typewriter is replaced by a new electric typewriter. The old typewriter is now valued at £35 in the accounts, but its resale value is only £5, so £30 is written off as depreciation.

At balancing time fixed assets are depreciated. A journal entry is made showing the depreciation. The fixed assets accounts are credited with the depreciation, then the amounts are posted to a composite depreciation account which is transferred to the profit and loss account as an expense against gross profit and shown on the balance sheet.

Example

On 31 December 19__ the fixed assets of the Truro Hotel were depreciated as follows:

1. Kitchen equipment £8000 (cost), 10 per cent depreciation.
2. Fixtures and fittings £15 000 (cost), £1500 depreciation.
3. China, plate and cutlery £5000 (cost), revalued at £3200 (£1800 depreciation).

J1

Date	Details	Folio	Debit £	Credit £
19__ Dec. 31	Depreciation account	L13	4100.00	
	Kitchen equipment (10 per cent)	L10		800.00
	Fixtures and fittings	L11		1500.00
	China, plate and cutlery	L12		1800.00
	Being depreciation written off			

Dr.   Kitchen Equipment (A/C no. 10)   Cr.

Date	Details	F	£	p	Date	Details	F	£	p
19__ Jan. 1	Balance	b/d	8000	00	19__ Dec. 31	Depreciation	J1	800	00
					31	Balance	c/d	7200	00
			8000	00				8000	00
19__ Jan. 1	Balance	b/d	7200	00					

Dr.   Fixtures and Fittings (A/C no. 11)   Cr.

Date	Details	F	£	p	Date	Details	F	£	p
19__ Jan. 1	Balance	b/d	15 000	00	19__ Dec. 31	Depreciation	J1	1 500	00
					31	Balance	c/d	13 500	00
			15 000	00				15 000	00
19__ Jan. 1	Balance	b/d	13 500	00					

Dr.   China, Plate and Cutlery (A/C no. 12)   Cr.

Date	Details	F	£	p	Date	Details	F	£	p
19__ Jan. 1	Balance	b/d	5000	00	19__ Dec. 31	Depreciation	J1	1800	00
					31	Balance	c/d	3200	00
			5000	00				5000	00
Jan. 1	Balance	b/d	3200	00					

Dr.   Depreciation (A/C no. 13)   Cr.

Date	Details	F	£	p	Date	Details	F	£	p
19__ Dec. 31	Kitchen equipment (10 per cent)	J1	800	00	19__ Dec. 31	Profit and loss A/C		4100	00
	Fixtures and fittings		1500	00					
	China, plate and cutlery		1800	00					
			4100	00				4100	00

Dr.   Profit and Loss Account for year ending 31 December 19__   Cr.

	£	£
Depreciation		
Kitchen equipment (10 per cent)	800.00	
Fixtures and fittings	1500.00	
China, plate and cutlery	1800.00	4100.00

Balance Sheet
as at 31 December 19_ _

		£	£
Fixed assets			
Freehold premises			125 000.00
Kitchen equipment		8 000.00	
Less depreciation		800.00	7 200.00
Fixtures and fittings		15 000.00	
Less depreciation		1 500.00	13 500.00
China, plate and cutlery		5 000.00	
Less depreciation		1 800.00	
Or revalued on_ _19_ _ at			3 200.00
			148 900.00

9.7   PROPRIETOR'S DRAWINGS

The owner's account in the book-keeping system is the capital account. If the proprietor wishes to draw funds from the business then a drawings account is opened and the amounts withdrawn are posted to the credit side of the cash book and to the debit side of the drawings account. The capital is the amount owed by the business to the owners, so before compiling the balance sheet any drawings would be deducted from the capital by debiting them to that account.

Example

During the course of the year the owner of the York Rose Hotel had drawings of £7000.

Dr.   Drawings (A/C no. 2)   Cr.

Date	Details	F	£	p	Date	Details	F	£	p
19_ _ Dec. 31	Total drawings	CB	7000	00					

Balance Sheet
as at 31 December 19__

	£	£
Capital	50 000	
Add net profit	15 000	
	65 000	
Less drawings	7 000	
		58 000

9.8   ALTERNATIVE 'T' PRESENTATION OF BALANCE SHEET

The method of presenting the balance sheet in 'T' form has become popular in recent years, as it reveals at a glance the total of fixed assets, the total of current assets, the working capital and net book value of fixed assets. The capital employed in the business is that which is contributed by the proprietor or shareholders plus any monies borrowed from other sources, i.e. loans, and this is equal to the net book value of the assets used in operating the business.

Example

Balance Sheet
as at 31 December 19___

	£	£	£
Fixed assets			
Freehold premises			225 000.00
Restaurant furniture	25 000.00		
Less depreciation	2 500.00		22 500.00
Kitchen equipment	15 000.00		
Less depreciation	1 500.00		13 500.00
Fixtures and fittings	17 000.00		
Less depreciation	1 700.00		15 300.00
China, plate and cutlery	3 000.00		
Less depreciation	300.00		2 700.00
			279 000.00
Current assets			
Stock	1 500.00		
Debtors	600.00		
Cash	400.00		
Bank	10 000.00		
		12 500.00	
Less current liabilities			
Sundry Creditors		2 500.00	
Working capital			10 000.00
Net book value of assets			289 000.00

	£
Capital	250 000.00
Add net profit	29 000.00
	279 000.00
Less drawings	10 000.00
	269 000.00
Long-term liability	
Loan from Smith and Co.	20 000.00
Capital employed	289 000.00

ASSIGNMENTS

A9.1 Explain the purpose of the trading account, the profit and loss account and the balance sheet.

A9.2 In which final account would the following ledger account balances appear?

(a) stock at end	(h) bank overdraft
(b) advertising	(i) laundry
(c) purchases returns (returns out)	(j) discounts received
(d) bank charges	(k) creditors
(e) bad debts	(l) cash in hand
(f) sales	(m) depreciation
(g) discounts allowed	(n) insurance

A9.3 Give two examples of each of the following:

(a) current assets;
(b) long-term liabilities;
(c) fixed assets;
(d) current liabilities

A9.4 (a) Define the term 'depreciation'.
(b) Give three main causes of depreciation.
(c) Explain what is meant by the following methods of depreciation:
  (i) the straight line method;
  (ii) the revaluation method;
  (iii) the diminishing balance method.

A9.5 The Suffolk Hotel had the following fixed assets as at 31 December 19__:

Leasehold premises £30 000 (20 years)
Fixtures and fittings £25 000 (cost)
China, plate, glass and cutlery £5000 (cost)

Show the journal entry, ledger accounts and balance sheet on 31 December 19__ when the fixed assets were depreciated as follows:

Leasehold premises: straight line method of writing a fixed sum
off the lease per annum
Fixtures and fittings: depreciate 10 per cent per annum
China, plate, glass and cutlery revalued to £3500

A9.6 Write explanatory notes on the treatment of staff meals and bad debts in the accounts system of a hotel.

A9.7 The following trial Balance was extracted from the accounts of the Primrose Hotel on 31 December 19__. Prepare the trading, profit and loss account and balance sheet and calculate the working capital.

Trial Balance
as at 31 December 19__

	Dr. £	Cr. £
Capital		298 080
Drawings	10 000	
Freehold premises	225 000	
Restaurant furniture	35 000	
Kitchen equipment	20 000	
Fixtures and fittings	19 000	
China, glass and cutlery	3 000	
Wages and salaries	54 600	
Heat, light and fuel	9 360	
Rates	6 300	
Insurance	1 700	
Repairs and renewals	1 550	
Sundry expenses	700	
Postage and telephone	3 100	
Banqueting debtor	420	
Sundry creditors		2 050
Purchases	82 250	
Returns out		350
Sales		195 000
Cash in hand	500	
Cash at bank	23 000	
	495 480	495 480

Stock at end £1750

Adjustments
Wages owing £1700
Rates prepaid £350

Depreciation
Restaurant furniture 10 per cent
Kitchen equipment 10 per cent
Fixtures and fittings 10 per cent
China, glass and cutlery revalued to £2250

A9.8 Prepare the trading account, profit and loss account and balance sheet and calculate the working capital from the following trial balance extracted at 30 June 19__ from the ledger accounts of the Hollyhock hotel.

Trial Balance as at
30 June 19__

	Dr. £	Cr. £
Sales		125 300
Net purchases	55 344	
Returns out		240
Discount received		150
Gas and electricity	3 500	
Fuel	3 000	
Advertising	700	
Printing and stationery	850	
Wages and salaries	33 430	
Postage and telephone	1 920	
Commission payable	240	
Commission received		120
Profit on currency exchange		180
Repairs and renewals	2 500	
Insurance	1 250	
Bank overdraft interest	1 500	
Sundry expenses	4 200	
Freehold premises	145 000	
Kitchen equipment	10 000	
Fixtures and fittings	22 000	
Restaurant furniture	12 000	
China, cutlery and linen	5 000	
Cash in hand	400	
Bank overdraft		10 000
Rates	5 200	
Bad debts	180	
Creditors		3 200
Banqueting debtors	520	
Capital		169 544
	308 734	308 734

Stock at 30 June 19__ £1100

Adjustments
Wages owing £920
Insurance prepaid £250

Depreciation
Kitchen equipment 10 per cent
Fixtures and fittings 10 per cent
Restaurant furniture 10 per cent
China, cutlery and linen revalued to £3500

A9.9 The following trial balance was extracted from the ledger accounts of the Bluebell Hotel on 31 March 19__ . Prepare the trading, profit and loss account and balance sheet and calculate the working capital, presenting the balance sheet in 'T' form.

Trial Balance
as at 31 March 19 __

	Dr. £	Cr. £
Capital		64 760
Stock 1 April	1 200	
Loan from Starmen Ltd		10 000
Sales		152 000
Net purchases	57 760	
Rent and rates	12 100	
Wages and salaries	47 120	
Gas and electricity	3 200	
Advertising	1 800	
Repairs and renewals	2 250	
Insurance	1 920	
Telephone	1 110	
Printing and stationery	740	
Kitchen equipment	17 500	
Restaurant furniture	9 500	
Fixtures and fittings	24 300	
China, glass and cutlery	3 400	
Banqueting debtors	630	
Creditors		3 240
Cash in hand	700	
Bank overdraft		15 000
Interest on loan	1 200	
Interest on bank overdraft	2 250	
Commission	170	
Rents received		350
Sundry expenses	1 500	
Leasehold premises	55 000	
	245 350	245 350

Stock 31 March £2750

Adjustments
Insurance prepaid £320
Rates prepaid £750
Wages owing £870

Depreciation
Kitchen equipment 10 per cent
Restaurant furniture 10 per cent
Fixtures and fittings 10 per cent
China, glass and cutlery revalued to £2800

10 Reports and Statistics

The financial information provided by the accounts system is used to measure and make comparisons of the performance and profitability of the business from one trading period to another.

Percentages, accounting ratios, statistics and reports are helpful in interpreting the accounts and presenting the operational information of the establishment in a simple manner which will aid and promote effective and profitable management decisions.

10.1   ACCOUNTING RATIOS

A ratio is simply a way of expressing the relationship between one figure and another. For example:

$$\frac{£25\ 000}{£100\ 000} = \text{a ratio of 1:4. Expressed as a percentage} \quad \frac{£25\ 000}{£100\ 000} \times \frac{100}{1} = 25 \text{ per cent}$$

$$\frac{£30\ 000}{£15\ 000} = \text{a ratio of 2:1. Expressed as a percentage} \quad \frac{£30\ 000}{£15\ 000} \times \frac{100}{1} = 200 \text{ per cent}$$

Management use percentages and ratios for continual comparisons, and the most important are those which are related to the profitability and liquidity of the business.

Profitability

Gross profit

This is usually expressed as a percentage of the sales. For example:

$$\frac{\text{Gross profit}}{\text{Sales}} = \frac{£78\ 000}{£120\ 000} \times \frac{100}{1} = 65 \text{ per cent}$$

Net Profit

This is usually expressed as a percentage of the sales. For example:

$$\frac{\text{Net profit}}{\text{Sales}} = \frac{£21\,600}{£120\,000} \times \frac{100}{1} = 18 \text{ per cent}$$

Liquidity

When measuring the liquidity of a business, the current assets less the current liabilities represents the 'working capital':

Current assets		Current liabilities		Working capital
£5000	−	£2000	=	£3000

The ratio is calculated as follows:

$$\frac{\text{Current assets}}{\text{Current liabilities}} = \frac{£5000}{£2000} = 5{:}2$$

Return on capital (net worth) invested

This can be expressed as a ratio or as a percentage:

$$\frac{\text{Net profit (after tax)}}{\text{capital (net worth)}} \quad \frac{£50\,000}{£250\,000} = 1{:}5 \;(20 \text{ per cent})$$

The acid test ratio

To calculate whether the business has sufficient liquid current assets, i.e. cash and debtors, to meet its current liabilities the 'acid test' ratio is applied. Stock is excluded from this calculation as its value cannot always be realized immediately.

$$\frac{\text{Current assets (less stock)}}{\text{Current liabilities}} = \frac{£30\,000}{£7\,500} = 4{:}1$$

Rate of stock turnover

To measure the buying efficiency of the establishment the rate at which the stock moves is measured by:

$$\frac{\text{Cost of sales}}{\substack{\text{Average stock} \\ \text{(at cost)}}} = \frac{£14\,000}{£3\,500} = 4{:}1 \;(\text{sometimes expressed as 4 times})$$

10.2   THE BASIC ELEMENTS OF COST

The hotelier and caterer are selling meals and accommodation services to the public and therefore their selling price must be fixed to cover the basic elements of cost, which are cost of
goods sold, labour costs, overheads and net profit. These costs are usually expressed as a percentage of the sales figure, and the accounts section provides the information for cost and
profit statements to be prepared for each revenue-producing department so that the percentages
can be studied and compared and, if necessary, action taken.

Example 1

The following information relating to the restaurant and bars for the year of 19__ was extracted from the accounts of the Bury Hotel.

	£
Sales	44 000
Purchases	18 500
Stock 1 January	6 200
Stock 31 December	5 800
Cost of staff meals	700
Purchases returns	600
Wages and expenses	19 100

From this information a cost and profit statement was prepared as follows:

Bury Hotel Restaurant and Bars
Cost and Profit Statement for the year ending 31 December 19__

	£	£	£	Percentage of sales
Sales			44 000	100
Stock 1 January		6 200		
Add purchases	18 500			
Less returns	600	17 900		
		24 100		
Less Stock 31 December		5 800		
		18 300		
Less staff meals		700		
Cost of goods sold			17 600	40
Gross profit			26 400	60
Wages and expenses			19 100	43.4
Net profit			7 300	16.6

Calculation of percentages:

$$\frac{\text{Cost of goods sold}}{\text{Sales}} = \frac{£17\ 600}{£44\ 000} \times \frac{100}{1} = 40 \text{ per cent}$$

$$\frac{\text{Staff meals}}{\text{Sales}} = \frac{£700}{£44\ 000} \times \frac{100}{1} = 1.6 \text{ per cent}$$

$$\frac{\text{Gross profit}}{\text{Sales}} = \frac{£26\ 400}{£44\ 000} \times \frac{100}{1} = 60 \text{ per cent}$$

$$\frac{\text{Wages and expenses}}{\text{Sales}} = \frac{£19\ 100}{£44\ 000} \times \frac{100}{1} = 43.4 \text{ per cent}$$

$$\frac{\text{Net profit}}{\text{Sales}} = \frac{£7300}{£44\,000} \times \frac{100}{1} = 16.6 \text{ per cent}$$

Formulae:

Sales	−	Cost of goods sold	=	Gross profit
£44 000		£17 600		£26 400
(100 per cent)		(40 per cent)		(60 per cent)
Gross profit	−	Wages and expenses	=	Net profit
£26 400		£19 100		£7300
(60 per cent)		(43.4 per cent)		(16.6 per cent)

Example 2

From the accounts section the following costs and expenses were attributed to the restaurant of the St Edmunds Hotel and a costs and profit statement was prepared for the month of June:

	£
Sales	4250
Stock 1 June	125
Stock 30 June	110
Purchases	1710
Returns to suppliers	25
Staff meals	170
Wages	1105
Heat, light and fuel	260
Repairs and maintenance	110
Cleaning materials	65
Depreciation	125
Sundry expenses	205

St Edmunds Hotel Restaurant
Cost and Profit Statement June 19_ _

	£	£	£	£	Percentage of sales
Sales				4250	100
Stock 1 June		125			
Purchases	1710				
Less returns	25	1685			
		1810			
Less stock 30 June		110			
		1700			
Less staff meals		170			
Cost of goods sold				1530	36
Gross profit				2720	64
Labour cost:					
Wages		1105			
Add staff meals		170	1275		30
Overheads:					
Heat, light and fuel		260			
Repairs and maintenance		110			
Cleaning materials		65			
Depreciation		125			
Sundry expenses		205	765		18
				2040	
Net profit				680	16

Calculation of percentages:

$$\frac{\text{Cost of goods sold}}{\text{Sales}} = \frac{£1530}{£4250} \times \frac{100}{1} = 36 \text{ per cent}$$

$$\frac{\text{Gross profit}}{\text{Sales}} = \frac{£2720}{£4250} \times \frac{100}{1} = 64 \text{ per cent}$$

$$\frac{\text{Labour cost}}{\text{Sales}} = \frac{£1275}{£4250} \times \frac{100}{1} = 30 \text{ per cent}$$

$$\frac{\text{Overheads}}{\text{Sales}} = \frac{£765}{£4250} \times \frac{100}{1} = 18 \text{ per cent}$$

$$\frac{\text{Net profit}}{\text{Sales}} = \frac{£680}{£4250} \times \frac{100}{1} = 16 \text{ per cent}$$

$$\frac{\text{Staff meals}}{\text{Sales}} = \frac{£170}{£4250} \times \frac{100}{1} = 4 \text{ per cent}$$

Formulae:

Sales	–	Cost of goods sold		= Gross profit
£4250		£1530		£2720
(100 per cent)		(36 per cent)		(64 per cent)
Gross profit	–	(Labour cost + Overheads)		= Net profit
£2720		(£1275 + £765) = £2040		£680
64 per cent		(30 per cent + 18 per cent) = 48 per cent	= 16 per cent

10.3   SALES MIX PERCENTAGES

The term 'sales mix' denotes how the total volume of sales is composed. Each component part is expressed as a percentage of the total and these percentages act as a guide to management on achieving maximum profitability and setting future targets.

Example 3

The sales mix for the Bath Hotel for the year ending 31 December 19__ was as follows:

	£
Room sales	36 120
Restaurant sales	25 585
Bar sales	12 040
Other sales	1 505
Total sales	75 250

Calculated as a percentage of total sales:

Room sales $\dfrac{\pounds 36\ 120}{\pounds 75\ 250} \times \dfrac{100}{1} = 48$ per cent

Restaurant sales $\dfrac{\pounds 25\ 585}{\pounds 75\ 250} \times \dfrac{100}{1} = 34$ per cent

Bar sales $\dfrac{\pounds 12\ 040}{\pounds 75\ 250} \times \dfrac{100}{1} = 16$ per cent

Other sales $\dfrac{\pounds 1505}{\pounds 75\ 250} \times \dfrac{100}{1} = 2$ per cent

After consideration of the sales mix percentages, a budget for the forthcoming year is to be prepared. It is estimated that:

1. A target of an 8 per cent increase on total sales should be set:

$$\frac{8}{100} \times \pounds 75\ 250 = \pounds 6020 + \pounds 75\ 250 = \pounds 81\ 270 \text{ sales target}$$

2. The sales mix is expected to vary as follows:

   (a) Room sales: an increase of 2 per cent = 50 per cent.
   (b) Restaurant sales: a decrease of 3 per cent = 31 per cent.
   (c) Bar sales: an increase of 2 per cent = 18 per cent.
   (d) Other sales: a decrease of 1 per cent = 1 per cent.

Solution

Department	Actual 19_ _ (£)	Percentage	Budget for next year (£)	Percentage
Room sales	36 120	48	40 635	50
Restaurant sales	25 585	34	25 194	31
Bar sales	12 040	16	14 629	18
Other sales	1 505	2	812	1
Total sales	75 250	100	81 270	100

10.4   LABOUR COST PERCENTAGES

The cost of employing staff in each individual department is an important statistic calculated as a percentage of the total wages bill, and as a percentage of the total sales.

Example 4

At the end of the year the following labour cost statement was prepared by the wages department:

Department	£	Percentage of total
Front office reception	14 625	15
Porterage	7 800	8
Housekeeping	29 250	30
Bars	6 825	7
Restaurant	17 550	18
Kitchen	21 450	22
Total wages	97 500	100

If the sales for the year were £325 000 then the total labour cost percentage would be:

$$\frac{\text{Total wages}}{\text{Sales}} \quad \frac{£97\ 500}{£325\ 000} \times \frac{100}{1} = 30 \text{ per cent}$$

If management forecast that in the forthcoming year sales will increase by 5 per cent and the labour cost percentage will increase by 2 per cent, the labour cost budget for each department will be as follows:

Sales + 5 per cent
£325 000 + £16 250 = £341 250 = Estimated sales for forthcoming year

Labour cost:

$$\frac{32}{100} \times £341\ 250 = £109\ 200$$

Departmental budgets for the forthcoming year:

Department	£	Percentage
Front office reception	16 380	15
Porterage	8 736	8
Housekeeping	32 760	30
Bars	7 644	7
Restaurant	19 656	18
Kitchen	24 024	22
Total	109 200	100

10.5 REPORTS

Departmental managers prepare regular reports on the operating efficiency of their individual revenue-producing departments.

Room occupancy report

This report (Fig. 10.1) is prepared daily and transferred to either a weekly or a monthly summary sheet (Fig. 10.2). To calculate an accurate room occupancy percentage, the number of

Room Occupancy Report

Date: 15th August 19__　　　　　Time: 2200

Floor 1			Floor 2			Floor 3			Floor 4			Floor 5		
Room no.	Let	No. of sleepers	Room no.	Let	No. of sleepers	Room no.	Let	No. of sleepers	Room no.	Let	No. of sleepers	Room no.	Let	No. of sleepers
101	✓	1	201	✓	1	301	✓	1	401	OOS		501	✓	1
102	✓	1	202	✓	1	302	✓	1	402			502	✓	1
103	✓	1	203	✓	1	303			403	✓	1	503	OOS	
104	OOS		204	✓	2	304			404	✓	2	504	OOS	
105	✓	2	205	✓	3	305			405			505	✓	2
106	✓	2	206			306	✓	2	406			506		
107	✓	2	207	✓	3	307	OOS		407	✓	2	507	OOS	
108			208			308	OOS		408	✓	2	508		
109	✓	2	209	OOS		309	✓	2	409			509	✓	2
110	✓	2	210	✓	2	310	OOS		410			510		
	8	**13**		**7**	**13**		**4**	**6**		**4**	**7**		**4**	**6**

(OOS = out of service)

Figure 10.1 *Room occupancy report.*

Maximum no. of rooms : 50		Maximum no. of sleepers : 85				
Floor	Maximum room occupancy	Actual room occupancy	Maximum no. of sleepers	Actual no. of sleepers	Room out of service
1	9	8	15	13	1
2	9	7	15	13	1
3	7	4	11	6	3
4	9	4	16	7	1
5	7	4	12	6	3
	41	27	69	45	9

Analysis:

Room occupancy percentage　　$\dfrac{27}{41} \times \dfrac{100}{1} = 65.8\%$

Bed occupancy percentage　　$\dfrac{45}{69} \times \dfrac{100}{1} = 65.2\%$

Room out of service percentage　　$\dfrac{9}{50} \times \dfrac{100}{1} = 18\%$

Sleeper loss percentage
(85−69 = 16)　　$= \dfrac{16}{85} \times \dfrac{100}{1} = 18.8\%$

Figure 10.2 *Summary sheet.*

rooms out of commission for either redecorating or repairs is deducted from the actual number of rooms available for letting in the hotel. For example:

Number of rooms in hotel	350
Less number of rooms not available for letting	18
Actual number of rooms available for letting	332
Number of rooms occupied	196

Room occupancy percentage:

$$\frac{196}{332} \times \frac{100}{1} = 59 \text{ per cent}$$

Bed occupancy report

A more accurate method of measuring whether the hotel is operating to its maximum capacity is to calculate the actual bed occupancy percentage:

$$\frac{\text{Number of sleepers}}{\text{Maximum guest capacity}} = \frac{356}{622} \times \frac{100}{1} = 57.2 \text{ per cent}$$

Double occupancy report

To measure the efficiency of the sale of double rooms the double occupancy percentage is calculated as follows:

$$\frac{\text{Number of sleepers occupying double rooms}}{\text{Maximum capacity of double rooms}} = \frac{540}{580} \times \frac{100}{1} = 93.1 \text{ per cent}$$

Date: Accommodation Analysis Report

Room type	Number available for letting	Actual let no.	Actual let %	Guest capacity	Actual number of guests no.	Actual number of guests %	Possible room sales £	Actual room sales £
Single	10	8	80	10	8	80	125.00	100·00
Single/bath	15	15	100	15	15	100	202.50	202·50
Twin	20	14	70	40	28	70	580.00	406·00
Twin/bath	40	38	95	80	76	95	1240.00	1178·00
Double	10	8	80	20	16	80	290.00	232·00
Double/bath	20	17	85	40	29	72·5	620.00	449·50
	115	100	87%	205	172	83·9	3057.50	2568·00

Analysis: $\dfrac{\text{Actual income}}{\text{Possible income}} = \dfrac{£2568.00}{£3057.50} \times \dfrac{100}{1} = 84\%$

Figure 10.3 *Accommodation analysis report.*

Daily room occupancy reports

These reports are completed daily by the housekeeping department for management to analyse.

Accommodation analysis report

The profitability of the accommodation operation is ascertained by studying the accommodation analysis report (Fig. 10.3).

10.6 METHODS OF CALCULATING AVERAGES

It is common practice to use averages when preparing statistics on guests' spending, room sales, lengths of stay of guests, etc. There are three types of average:

1. Mean. To calculate the mean, divide the total by the number of weeks it represents.
2. Median. To calculate the median, arrange the figures in either ascending or descending order and select the middle figure. If the number of figures is odd, this is easy. However, if the number is even, add the two middle figures together and then divide by two, i.e. find the mean of the two middle figures.
3. Mode. This is the name given to the most frequently repeated figure in the series.

For example:

	Arithmetical mean	*Median*	*Mode*
Week no.	Room sales	Room sales in descending order	*The most frequently repeated number
	£	£	£
1	2500	2750	2500
2	2550	2700	2550
3	2400	2650	2400
4	2500	2600	2500
5	2600	2600	2600*
6	2750	2600	2750
7	2700	2550	2700
8	2650	2550	2650
9	2600	2520	2600*
10	2550	2500	2550
11	2600	2500	2600*
12	2520	2400	2520

Mean = £30 920 ÷ 12 = £2577

$$\text{Median} = \frac{£2600 + £2550}{2} = £2575$$

Mode = *£2600 (3 times)

10.7 USE OF PIE CHARTS, BAR CHARTS AND GRAPHS

Charts and graphs are a method of presenting statistical information in a simple visual form.

The sales mixes for the Eagle Hotel for the four quarters of the year 19__ were as shown in Table 10.1.

Table 10.1   *Sales mix 19__*

Department	First quarter £	%	Second quarter £	%	Third quarter £	%	Fourth quarter £	%
Room sales	7 260	44	9 360	52	9 500	50	7 130	46
Restaurant sales	6 930	42	6 480	36	7 220	38	6 200	40
Bar and other sales	2 310	14	2 160	12	2 280	12	2 170	14
Total sales	16 500	100	18 000	100	19 000	100	15 500	100

This information can be expressed as a pie chart (Fig. 10.4), as a bar chart (Fig. 10.5), or as a graph (Fig. 10.6).

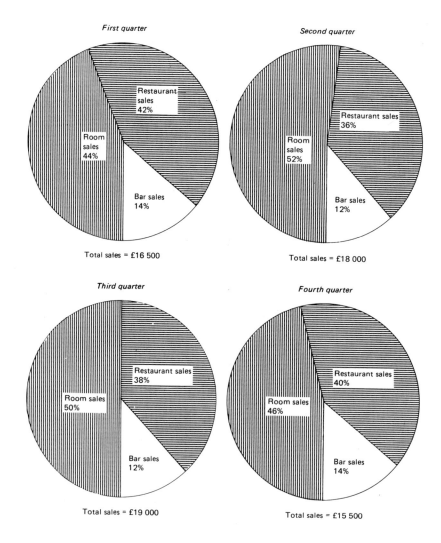

Figure 10.4 *Sales mix expressed as a pie chart.*

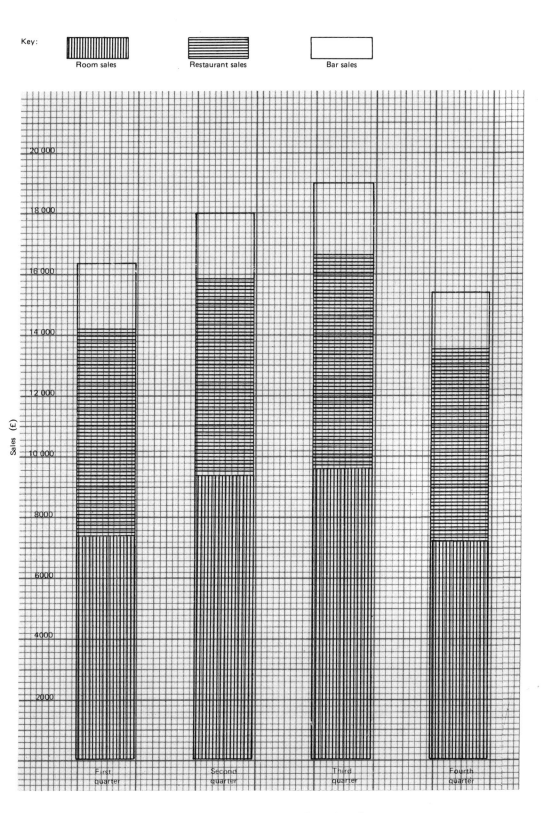

Figure 10.5 *Sales mix expressed as a bar chart.*

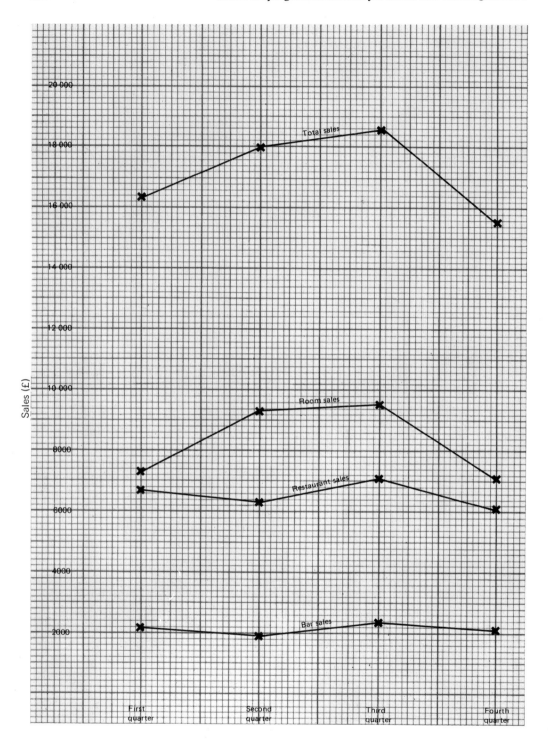

Figure 10.6 *Sales mix expressed as a graph.*

ASSIGNMENTS

A10.1 Express the following figures as ratios and as percentages:

(a) $\dfrac{£75\ 000}{£225\ 000}$

(b) $\dfrac{£70\ 000}{£105\ 000}$

(c) $\dfrac{£80\ 000}{£60\ 000}$

A10.2 Complete the following table:

Unit	Sales	Cost of goods sold	%	Gross profit margin	Gross profit
	£	£		£	%
1	55 000	20 900			
2	82 000			52 480	
3	74 500	29 800			
4	102 300			66 495	
5	63 200	23 384		_____	_____
Total					

A10.3 Complete the following table:

Unit	Current assets	Current liabilities	Working capital	Ratio
	£	£	£	
1	7200	2400		
2	2100	1400		
3	900	1200		
4	6400	3200		
5	2250	3750	_____	_____
Total				

A10.4 Explain what you understand by the following terms:

(a) the acid ratio test;
(b) rate of stock turnover;
(c) the basic elements of cost.

A10.5 From the following information extracted from the accounts of the Swallow Hotel prepare a cost and profit statement for the restaurant for the month of June, expressing each element of cost as a percentage of sales:

	£
Sales	5250
Stock 1 June	110
Stock 30 June	95
Purchases	2065
Returns	25

Heat, light and fuel	180
Cleaning and laundry	85
Repairs and renewals	75
Sundry expenses	290
Depreciation	210
Wages	1620
Staff meals	60

A10.6 Prepare from the following information a cost and profit statement for the month of August, expressing each element of cost as a percentage of sales:

Robin Hotel Restaurant
August 19_ _

	£
Stock 1 August	142
Purchases	3064
Returns	20
Stock 31 August	102
Staff meals	120
Restaurant wages	1420
Kitchen wages	816
Heat, light and fuel	365
Cleaning materials	30
Repairs and renewals	105
Insurances	45
Sundry expenses	325
Depreciation	250
Sales	7600

A10.7 The following figures were extracted from the accounts relating to the restaurant of the Wagtail Hotel. Prepare two half-yearly statements showing:

(i)   the half-year gross profit;
(ii) the gross profit as a percentage of sales;
(iii) the half-year net profit;
(iv) the net profit as a percentage of sales;
(v)   the cost of staff meals as a percentage of sales.

(a)   *1 Jan.–30 June 19_ _*

	£
Sales	21 000
Purchases	8 140
Stock 1 January	1 000
Stock 30 June	800
Value of goods returned to suppliers	150
Cost of staff meals	600
Labour costs and expenses	7 800

(b)   *1 July – 31 Dec. 19_ _*

	£
Sales	18 000
Purchases	7 180
Stock 1 July	800
Stock 31 December	1 210
Cost of staff meals	670
Purchases returns	140
Labour costs and expenses	7 250

A10.8 The sales mix for the Flamingo Hotel for the year ending 31 December 19_ _ was as follows:

Department	£
Room sales	105 750
Restaurant sales	78 750
Bar sales	29 250
Other sales	11 250

For the forthcoming year a target of a 5 per cent increase on sales is to be set, and the sales mix is expected to vary as follows:

(i)   room sales will increase by 6 per cent;
(ii) restaurant sales will decrease by 2 per cent;
(iii) bar sales will decrease by 1 per cent;
(iv) other sales will decrease by 3 per cent.

From this information prepare a sales budget for the forthcoming year.

A10.9 The sales mix of the Seagull Hotel for the year ending 31 December 19_ _ was as follows:

Department	£
Room sales	204 240
Restaurant sales	119 140
Bar sales	63 825
Other sales	38 295

For the forthcoming year a target of a 7 per cent increase on sales is to be set, and the sales mix will vary as follows:

(i)   room sales will increase by 3 per cent;
(ii) restaurant sales will increase by 2 per cent;
(iii) bar sales will decrease by 1 per cent;
(iv) other sales will decrease by 4 per cent.

From this information prepare a sales budget for the forthcoming year.

A10.10 At the end of the year the following labour cost statement was prepared by the wages department of the Pelican Hotel:

Department	£
Front office reception	14 756
Porterage	6 076
Housekeeping	21 700
Bars	8 680
Restaurant	16 492
Kitchen	19 096

The sales for the year amounted to £310 000. The management forecast that sales will increase by 7 per cent and total labour costs will increase by 3 per cent in the forthcoming year. From this information prepare the labour cost budget for the coming year, assuming that the departmental percentages will remain constant.

A10.11 The following departmental labour costs were prepared by the accounts section of the Swan Hotel for the year 19__:

Department	£
Front office reception	11 964
Porterage	4 785
Housekeeping	21 534
Bar	9 570
Restaurant	14 356
Kitchen	17 546

The sales for the year amounted to £265 850. The management estimate that sales will increase by 10 per cent and labour costs will increase by 3 per cent in the forthcoming year. Assuming that departmental labour costs percentages will remain constant, prepare the labour cost budget for the forthcoming year.

A10.12 Complete the following room occupancy report.

Room Occupancy Report

Maximum number of rooms: 40
Maximum number of sleepers: 68

Date: 5 March 19__
Time: 2200

Floor 1				Floor 2				Floor 3				Floor 4			
Room no.	Type	Let	No. of sleepers	Room no.	Type	Let	No. of sleepers	Room no.	Type	Let	No. of sleepers	Room no.	Type	Let	No. of sleepers
101	D	✓	2	201	D			301	D	✓	2	401	D		
102	D	✓	2	202	D	OOS		302	D	OOS		402	D		
103	Tw	✓		203	Tw	✓	2	303	Tw	✓	2	403	Tw	✓	2
104	Tw	✓	3	204	Tw	✓	2	304	Tw	✓	3	404	Tw	OOS	
105	Tw	✓	2	205	Tw			305	Tw	✓	3	405	Tw	OOS	
106	Tw	✓	2	206	Tw	✓	2	306	Tw			406	Tw	✓	2
107	Tw	✓	1	207	Tw	OOS		307	Tw			407	Tw		
108	S			208	S	✓	1	308	S	✓	1	408	S		
109	S	OOS		209	S	✓	1	309	S	✓	1	409	S	✓	1
110	S	✓	1	210	S	✓	1	310	S	✓	1	410	S		

Summary

Analysis:

Room occupancy percentage
Bed occupancy percentage
Rooms out of service percentage
Sleeper loss percentage

A10.13 The tariff for the Falcon Hotel is as follows:

Rates per person per day	£
Single room	20.50
Single room with bath	23.00
Twin	20.00
Twin with bath	22.50
Double	19.00
Double with bath	21.50

Using the above rates, complete the following accommodation analysis report.

Room type	Available for let	Actual let		Guest capacity	Actual no. of guests		Possible sales	Actual sales
	no.	no.	%	no.	no.	%	£	£
Single	2	2		2	2			
Single/bath	4	3		4	3			
Twin	5	2		10	4			
Twin/bath	20	15		40	30			
Double	4	1		8	2			
Double/bath	15	12		30	24			
Totals								

$$\frac{\text{Actual income}}{\text{Possible income}} = \frac{£}{£} \times \frac{100}{1} = \quad \%$$

A10.14 Complete the following statements and prepare pie charts, bar charts or graphs from the statistical information.

(a)

Sales Mix 19__

Department	First quarter £	%	Second quarter £	%	Third quarter £	%
Room sales	65 000		60 960		59 800	
Restaurant sales	46 250		49 530		52 000	
Bar sales	11 250		13 970		15 600	
Other sales	2 500		2 540		2 600	
Totals						

(b)

Statement of Costs and Profits

	First quarter £	%	Second quarter £	%	Third quarter £	%
Fixed costs	33 750		33 740		33 785	
Variable costs	56 700		58 800		60 900	
Semi-variable costs	24 300		22 260		21 315	
Net profit						
Sales	135 000		140 000		145 000	

(c)

Statement of Costs and Profits

	First quarter £	%	Second quarter £	%	Third quarter £	%
Food cost	1750		2090		2320	
Labour cost	1600		1540		1740	
Overheads	1150		1100		1044	
Net profit						
Sales	5000		5500		5800	

11 Mechanized and Computerized Hotel Accounting Systems

As the hotel and catering industry continues to grow internationally the need for improved services, immediate and up-to-the-minute information on the availability of accommodation, and complete management control over the complex accounting records has prompted the development of many sophisticated computerized guest accounting systems.

It is not possible to go into the details of all the computerized systems on the market, but just a few of those used in the industry are the NCR series, the Sweda International electronic cash registers, and the Hoskyns hotel accounting systems.

11.1   THE NCR 2251

This system is a free-standing, electronic, front-desk terminal (Fig. 11.1) which enables management to simplify posting procedures. Every transaction is monitored from the time a guest checks in to the time the bill is settled.

The keyboard is flexible in design and has numerical key arrangements, department keys, settlement keys and an assortment of special-function keys located conveniently for minimum operator error.

Departmental totals

Departmental keys (Fig. 11.2) permit separate totals for guest services, room charge, restaurant and bar services, valet, laundry, florist, garage and others.

Cashier accountability

Three cashier identification keys are provided and cashier or shift identification is printed on folios (bills), vouchers and audit journals. A compulsory signing-on procedure ensures maximum cash control and prevents unauthorized operation of the terminal.

Figure 11.1   *The NCR 2251. Reproduced with the permission of NCR Ltd.*

Errors

Posting errors are corrected using the correction key or void key. Correct totals are accumulated to give complete management control.

Room rates

Room rates are stored in the memory of the computer. The cashier enters the room rate code and presses the room-rate look-up key. The terminal locates the rate in its memory, prints the room-rate charge on the folio and updates the totals.

Figure 11.2 *The NCR 2251 showing departmental keys. Reproduced with the permission of NCR Ltd.*

Package plan arrangements

When accommodation and services are offered at special rates, the computer can distribute the charges automatically to their respective revenue department totals. This information prints on the audit journal but only the total package price prints on the guest's folio (bill).

Room number and balance pick-up verification

Electronic check-digit verification of room number and previous balance pick-up eliminate a common error in posting guest folios. An automatic check digit is generated each time a new balance prints; when room number and balance pick-up check digits are entered, room number and balance pick-up are verified electronically and, if incorrect, the terminal rejects the entire entry as invalid.

Advance payments

On check-in an advance payment can be transferred from the advance reservation deposit account by using the transfer debit and transfer credit key.

Trial balance

Under supervisory control the trial balance feature provides automatic accumulation of new debit and credit balances in separate totals. This simplifies the night audit procedures and ensures accuracy.

11.2   THE HOSKYNS COMPUTER SYSTEMS FOR HOTELS

The Hoskyns Group offer a range of computer systems, from those suitable for hotels with 25–125 bedrooms up to the main Hoskyns hotel system designed for hotels with 100–500 bedrooms (Fig. 11.3). Apart from all the usual features necessary for guest accounting, the computerized system will also provide:

Figure 11.3   *Hoskyns computer systems for hotels: Gatwick Post House.*
Reproduced with the permission of the Hoskyns Group Ltd.

(a)

(b)

Figure 11.4 *(a) The visual display used for advance reservations and guest check-in. (b) Close-up of room status display. Reproduced with the permission of the Hoskyns Group Ltd.*

1. Full automatic apartment charging.
2. Automatic analysis of inclusive terms.
3. Guest lists.
4. Departure lists.
5. Room status lists.
6. Room/sleeper sales statistics.
7. VAT analysis.
8. Reservation lists (Fig. 11.4).
9. Room availability reports.
10. Forward book analysis.

Cashier terminals

The cashier terminals designed to operate in conjunction with the hotel system provide:

1. Bill settlement and other payments in any combination of cash, cheques, traveller's cheques or credit cards with automatic sterling conversion.
2. Foreign currency exchange using up to 16 present rates.
3. Automatic posting of payments or other transactions directly to guests' accounts in the hotel system.
4. Detailed analysis of cash drawer totals, cashier totals and banking totals.
5. Fully itemized receipts for customers.

Restaurant terminals

The restaurant terminals (Fig. 11.5) can operate in three ways:

1. As a stand-alone device.
2. As an extension to the hotel system.
3. As part of a communication network.

Special features

Waiter operation:

1. Tracks and controls all items ordered.
2. Machine-printed requisitions giving quantity, description and comment.
3. Direct link to kitchen.
4. Fast, simple end-of-shift balancing.
5. Automatic production of bill.

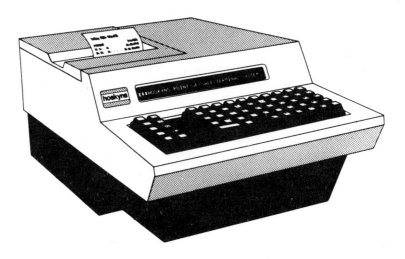

Figure 11.5 *Hoskyns restaurant terminal. Reproduced with the permission of the Hoskyns Group Ltd.*

Cashier operation:

1. Automatic pricing for speed and accuracy.
2. Simple lead-through operation.
3. Operator recognition by individual key.
4. Several bills per table.
5. Detailed quality bill for presentation.

For the customer:

1. A quality bill.
2. Full description of items.
3. Portions shown to eliminate queries.
4. Always accurately totalled.
5. Easily changeable hospitality message.

Used in conjunction with hotel system:

1. Up-to-the-minute direct posting to guests' accounts.
2. Validation of guests' names and room status.

For administration and management:

1. Operating and performance analysis.
2. Individual order print-out.
3. Portion total and revenue.
4. Cover analysis.
5. Waiter performance by cover and by amount spent on food and wine.
6. Cashier security and accuracy.
7. Individual cashier control.
8. Spread sheet.
9. Payment method analysis.
10. Full audit trail.

11.3   SWEDA L-45-30

This electronic cash register (Fig. 11.6) has been specially tailored for the hotel industry and offers some of the following features:

1. Forty departments to cover such services as laundry, telephone, restaurant, bar, etc.
2. Eleven types of payment. Eight miscellaneous keys cover major credit cards, all with programmable limitations to alert the operator when management authorization must be given to accept vouchers over a certain amount.
3. Room balance: up to 512 room balances may be stored.
4. Training mode used for cashier training.
5. Currency conversion.
6. Debit and credit balances.
7. VAT system.
8. Guest and ledger trial balances to facilitate complete hotel accounting.
9. Folio printer in four columns. Reference, debit credit balancing to any entry.
10. Alpha-numerical display to let the cashier know when to insert vouchers etc.
11. 93–108 price look-ups.

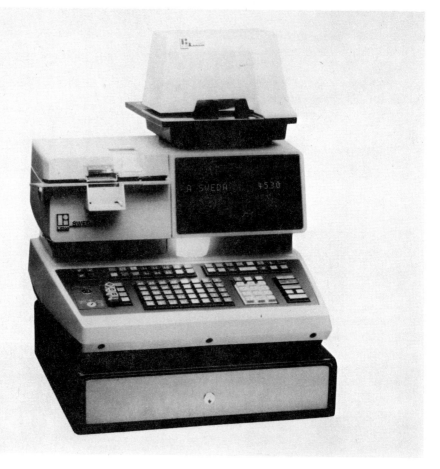

Figure 11.6 *Sweda L-45-30. Reproduced with the permission of Sweda International.*

12. Room-number entry system with automatic balance pick-up.
13. Communication package for transfer of guest charges from one room folio to another.
14. Guest name file where the first four characters of a guest's name are written on the charge sheet for posting to the folio, which has to be verified before being accepted.
15. Cassette for data recording.

11.4   SOFTWARE PROGRAMS

Many companies specialize in designing programs (software) for microcomputers (hardware). If programmed correctly, the computer will be able to do the following automatically:

1. It can recognize the date and charges to the guests' accounts, e.g. morning beverages and newspapers.
2. By entering the room number the guest's account can be brought to the screen immediately.
3. The list of possible service items can be whatever the individual hotel requires. Some items may be set at zero-rated VAT.

4. The copy bills can stay in a continuous strip, thus providing an accurate detail of operations.
5. Provision can be made for prepaid deposits.
6. Payment can be accepted by cash, cheque, credit cards or a mixture of these.
7. Changes can be made to guests' names, room numbers, or rate of accommodation or meals, and items can be deleted from an account.
8. The totals of any deleted items can be recorded on the total analysis for control purposes.
9. When accounts have been altered another account is usually printed before the amount of the payment is indicated and the account closed.
10. Daily totals and period totals can be called to the screen when required and printed, if necessary, by using a security code to prevent unauthorized viewing. These would include:

    (a) accommodation;
    (b) service items;
    (c) credit totals;
    (d) total including service charge;
    (e) payment by credit card;
    (f) prepayments and total deposits;
    (g) outstanding debt to the hotel at that time;
    (h) total of deleted items.

    The totals automatically zero at each date change, and provision can be made to change the VAT rate or service charge rate.
11. When a new guest is registered the following details are obtained:

    (a) the room number;
    (b) the guest's name;
    (c) the daily accommodation rate;
    (d) breakfast, lunch and dinner charges;
    (e) morning beverage and newspapers;
    (f) deposit.

    This information is fed into the computer and the computer can work out a period charge or, more usually, the account can show the daily charge. The computer will file the information and open an account. If the room is already occupied the computer displays the fact when anyone tries to register the room number.
12. The guest register can be called in and displays room numbers and guests' names in ascending order.
13. The computer can give an automatic printout of all bills on file at the touch of a key.

These systems are exceptionally easy to use and receptionist training is a matter of only a few hours.

ASSIGNMENTS

A11.1   Explain the advantages and disadvantages of computerized hotel accounting systems.

A11.2   What do you understand by the following terms:

(a) hardware;
(b) software?

A11.3   Computerized guest accounts systems are capable of performing many operations including producing management data, information and statistics. Give details of these operations.

A11.4   Explain some of the features of:

(a) a cashier terminal;
(b) a restaurant terminal.

A11.5   As a project gather material and information on the following:

(a) other computerized hotel systems;
(b) inter-hotel systems;
(c) Holidex;
(d) Trusthouse Forte's Guestel system;
(e) Prestel;
(f) Roomwatch.

ANSWERS TO ASSIGNMENTS

The following answers are only a guide. Full accounting statements are not reproduced, but are available in a separate lecturer's guide. Students should refer to the relevant sections of the text to check the form that these statements actually take.

Chapter 1

A1.1
to   *See Chapter 1.*
A1.3

Chapter 2

A2.1   *See Chapter 2.*

A2.2

	Account to be debited	Account to be credited
(a)	Purchases (Provisions)	Cash
(b)	Rent	Bank
(c)	Cash	Sales
(d)	Kitchen equipment	B. Fine Ltd
(e)	Insurance	Bank
(f)	Purchases (provisions)	B. Grape Ltd
(g)	China, plate and glass	Bank
(h)	Advertising	Bank
(i)	Wages	Cash
(j)	Bank	Capital

A2.3

(a)	Nominal	(k)	Real
(b)	Nominal	(l)	Nominal
(c)	Nominal	(m)	Personal
(d)	Real	(n)	Real
(e)	Nominal	(o)	Nominal
(f)	Nominal	(p)	Real
(g)	Real	(q)	Nominal
(h)	Real	(r)	Real
(i)	Personal	(s)	Nominal
(j)	Nominal	(t)	Real

A2.4   L. Sleet A/C: Balance 31 March   Cr. £160
                                Balance 30 April   Cr. £205
A2.5   M. Flower A/C: Balance 31 January Dr. £200
                                Balance 28 February Dr £74

A2.6   *See Chapter 2.*
A2.7   Trial balance totals Dr./Cr. £130 300
A2.8   Trial balance totals Dr./Cr. £135 014
A2.9   Gross profit £67 460; net profit £17 780; balance sheet totals £304 650
A2.10   Gross profit £79 050; net profit £21 400; balance sheet totals £155 370

Chapter 3

A3.1   (a)–(j)(i)   *See Chapter 3.*

	(j)(ii)		
		Total cash	£376.77
		Total cheques	76.50
		Total paid in	£453.27

A3.2   31 March   Cash balance   £138
                        Bank balance   £1002
A3.3   12 January Cash balance   £3
                        Bank balance   £902.50
A3.4   7 January   Cash balance   £417
                        Bank balance   £4372

A3.5	7 January	Cash balance	£216.25
		Bank balance	£4990.80
A3.6	7 January	Cash balance	£390
		Bank balance	£2115.50
	14 January	Cash balance	£25
		Bank balance	£3269
A3.7	5 March	Petty cash balance	£3.63
		Reimbursing cheque	£11.37
A3.8	17 January	Petty cash balance	£5.70
		Reimbursing cheque	£34.30
A3.9	*See Chapter 3.*		
A3.10	14 January	Petty cash balance	£1.20
		Reimbursing cheque	£28.80
	22 January	Petty cash balance	£2.20
		Reimbursing cheque	£27.80
A3.11	*See Chapter 3.*		

A3.12   *Bank Reconciliation Statement as at 31 March 19— —*

	£	£
Balance as per cash book (Dr.)		2635.56
Add cheques not yet presented	280.36	
Bank giro credit	200.00	480.36
		3115.92
Less cheques not yet credited		
Budd Ltd	92.00	
Sales	510.00	
Standing order	160.00	
Bank charges	16.42	778.42
Balance as per Bank Statement (Cr.)		2337.50

A3.13	*See section 3.29.*
A3.14	*See section 3.29.*
A3.15	*Answers according to current exchange rates.*

Chapter 4

A4.1	*See Chapter 4.*		
A4.2	*September*		
	Purchases daybook total		£479.60
	Purchases returns daybook total		£23.10
	October		
	Purchases daybook total		£395.50
	Purchases returns daybook total		£11.70
	Ledger balances: 1 October	A. Wine Co. Ltd	£184.40
		Fish Bros	£138.40
		A. Butcher and Sons	£133.70
	Ledger balances: 1 November	A. Wine Co. Ltd	£205.40
		Fish Bros	£104.70
		A. Butcher and Sons	£73.70
A4.3	Sales daybook total		£236.65
	Ledger balances 1 October	C. Breezy Ltd	£81.60
		A. Summer Ltd	£75.50
		Winter Glass Co.	£66.55
	Total allowances		£13.00
	Total cash receipts		£229.00
A4.4	*Special functions daybook totals*		
	Food	£2120.00	
	Tobacco and liquor	£293.00	
	Total	£2413.00	
	Total cash receipts	£2292.34	
	Total discounts allowed	£120.66	
	Total	£2413.00	

A4.5	(a)	1 November	Balance b/d (Total creditors)		£935.00		
	(b)	1 November	Balance b/d (Total debtors)		£628.00		
A4.6		1 July	Cash balance b/d	£3935.00			
			Bank balance b/d	£30 830.00			
		30 June	Purchases daybook total		£2060.00		
			Purchases return daybook total		£55.00		
		30 June	Trial balance totals		£260 430.00		
			Gross profit		£2865.00		
			Net profit		£1260.00		
			Balance sheet totals		£257 265.00		

A4.7	(a)		VAT inclusive	VAT	Total	Service charge	VAT exclusive
		Totals	986.58	128.68	857.90	95.34	762.56

	(b)		VAT inclusive	VAT	Total	Service charge	VAT exclusive
		Totals	522.27	68.12	454.15	50.47	403.68

Chapter 5

A5.1	*See Chapter 5.*			
A5.2	(a)	Capital	£305 330	
		Journal totals	£307 250	
	(b)	Capital	£77 010	
		Journal totals	£103 570	
A5.3	March	1	Kitchen equipment A/C	debit
			Glencoe Co. Ltd A/C	credit
		7	Glencoe Co. Ltd A/C	debit
			Kitchen equipment A/C	credit
		14	Office equipment A/C	debit
			McKay Co. A/C	credit
		14	McKay Co. A/C	debit
			Office equipment A/C	credit
		15	Office Furniture A/C	debit
			B. McTavish A/C	credit
		15	China, plate and cutlery A/C	debit
			McLaren Ltd A/C	credit
A5.4	April	1	B. Gregory A/C	debit
			B. McGregor A/C	credit
		5	Purchases A/C	debit
			Suspense A/C	credit (See Chapter 8)
		17	V. Stewart A/C	debit
			V. Stone A/C	credit
		17	China and cutlery A/C	debit
			Purchases A/C	credit
		30	Discount allowed A/C	debit
			Discount received A/C	credit
		30	Sales A/C	debit
			Suspense A/C	credit (See Chapter 8)
A5.5	June	1	Drawing A/C	debit
			Purchases A/C	credit
		2	S. McInnes A/C	debit
			Discount allowed A/C	credit
		7	Discount received A/C	debit
			McKay Co. Ltd A/C	credit
A5.6	March	31	Sales A/C	debit
			Trading A/C	credit
		31	Trading A/C	debit
			Purchases A/C	credit
		31	Purchases returns A/C	debit
			Trading A/C	credit

31	Profit and loss A/C	debit
	Postage and stationery A/C	credit
31	Profit and loss A/C	debit
	Gas and electricity	credit
31	Profit and loss A/C	debit
	Wages A/C	credit

A5.7   *Opening journal entry*
1 January Capital £185 870
Totals £186 320
Trial balance totals £187 460
Final accounts
Gross profit £380
Net profit £120
Balance sheet totals £186 930

Chapter 6

A6.1   *See Chapter 6.*
A6.2   *See Chapter 6.*
A6.3   *See Chapter 6.*

A6.4   *Bellair Hotel*

	£
Daily total	1679.01
Brought forward	557.55
Total debits	2236.56
Allowances	2.40
Cash received	702.57
Transferred to ledger	1066.22
Carried forward	465.37
Total credits	2236.56

A6.5   *Cavender Hotel*

	£
Daily total	534.43
Brought forward	344.57
Total debits	879.00
Allowances	0.95
Cash received	574.00
Transferred to ledger	267.48
Carried forward	36.57
Total credits	879.00

A6.6   *Royal Hotel*

	£
Daily total	501.93
Brought forward	320.82
Total debits	822.75
Allowances	10.75
Cash received	286.46
Transferred to ledger	318.22
Carried forward	207.22
Total credits	822.75

A6.7   *Jamesville Hotel*

	£
Daily total	855.65
Brought forward	321.79
Total debits	1177.44
Allowances	1.50
Cash received	323.05
Transferred to ledger	399.60
Carried forward	453.29
Total credits	1177.44

A6.8   *Dalton Hotel*

	£
Daily total	699.46
Brought forward	199.37
Total debits	898.83
Allowances	1.75
Cash received	540.81
Transferred to ledger	193.55
Carried forward	162.72
Total credits	898.83

A6.9   *Glanville Hotel*

	£
Daily total	626.44
Brought forward	142.35
Total debits	768.79
Allowances	0.65
Cash received	373.59
Transferred to ledger	240.50
Carried forward	154.05
Total credits	768.79

Chapter 7

A7.1
to
A7.7   *See Chapter 7.*

A7.8

		£ p
Cash analysis	60 x £10 =	600.00
	8 x £5 =	40.00
	23 x £1 =	23.00
	7 x 50p =	3.50
	10 x 20p =	2.00
	6 x 10p =	0.60
	8 x 5p =	0.40
	9 x 2p =	0.18
	4 x 1p =	0.04
	Total	669.72

A7.9
to
A7.11   *See Chapter 7.*

Chapter 8

A8.1
to
A8.5   *See Chapter 8.*

A8.6		£
	Totals of trial balance	248 330
	Gross profit	78 440
	Net profit	31 000
	Balance sheet totals	158 580
A8.7		£
	Totals of trial balance	235 140
	Gross profit	105 910
	Net profit	31 175
	Balance sheet totals	104 550
A8.8		£
	Totals of trial balance	141 920
	Gross profit	49 780
	Net profit	11 110
	Balance sheet totals	72 530
A8.9		£
	Totals of trial balance	266 600
	Gross profit	63 630
	Net profit	10 540
	Balance sheet totals	166 550

A8.10 Journal entries:

March 31	Suspense A/C	debit
	Difference in trial balance	credit
April 30	Purchases returns A/C	debit
	Suspense A/C	credit
	Discount allowed A/C	debit
	Suspense A/C	credit
	Suspense A/C	debit
	R. White A/C	credit
	Cash A/C	debit
	Suspense A/C	credit

A8.11 Journal entries:

Dec. 31	Difference in trial balance	debit
	Suspense A/C	credit
Jan. 31	Advertising A/C	debit
	Suspense A/C	credit
	Suspense A/C	debit
	Sales A/C	credit
	Suspense A/C	debit
	M. Horton A/C	credit
	Purchases A/C	debit
	Suspense A/C	credit
Feb. 1	Balance of suspense A/C	credit £100

Chapter 9

A9.1 *See Chapter 9.*

A9.2

(a) Trading balance sheet	(h) Balance sheet
(b) Profit and loss	(i) Profit and loss
(c) Trading	(j) Profit and loss
(d) Profit and loss	(k) Balance sheet
(e) Profit and loss	(l) Balance sheet
(f) Trading	(m) Profit and loss balance sheet
(g) Profit and loss	(n) Profit and loss

A9.3 *See Chapter 9.*

A9.4 *See Chapter 9.*

A9.5 Journal entry:

Depreciation A/C debit	£5500
Leasehold premises credit	£1500
Fixtures and fittings credit	£2500
China, plate, glass and cutlery credit	£1500

Dr. *Balance Sheet as at 31 December 19_ _* Cr.

		£	£
Fixed assets			
Leasehold premises		30 000	
Less depreciation		1 500	28 500
Fixtures and fittings		25 000	
Less depreciation		2 500	22 500
China, plate, glass and cutlery		5 000	
Less depreciation		1 500	3 500
			54 500

A9.6   *See Chapter 9.*

A9.7

Gross profit	£114 850
Net profit	£28 040
Working capital	£22 270

A9.8

Gross profit	£71 296
Net profit	£6 706
Working capital	£11 850

A9.9

Gross profit	£95 790
Net profit	£15 250
Working capital	£13 960

Chapter 10

A10.1

(a)   1:3; $33\frac{1}{3}$ per cent
(b)   2:3; 66.6 per cent
(c)   4:3; 133.3 per cent

A10.2

Unit	Sales £	Cost of goods sold £	%	Gross profit margin £	Gross profit %
1	55 000	20 900	38	34 100	62
2	82 000	29 520	36	52 480	64
3	74 500	29 800	40	44 700	60
4	102 300	35 805	35	66 495	65
5	63 200	23 384	37	39 816	63
Total	377 000	139 409	37	237 591	63

A10.3

Unit	Current assets £	Current liabilities £	Working capital £	Ratio
1	7 200	2 400	4800	3:1
2	2 100	1 400	700	3:2
3	900	1 200	−300	3:4
4	6 400	3 200	3200	2:1
5	2 250	3 750	−1500	3:5
	18 850	11 950	6900	1.58:1

A10.4   *See Chapter 10.*

A10.5

	£	
Cost of goods sold	1955	37.2 per cent
Gross profit	3295	62.8 per cent
Labour costs	1680	32.0 per cent
Overheads	840	16.0 per cent
Net profit	775	14.8 per cent

A10.6

	£	
Cost of goods sold	2964	39.0 per cent
Gross profit	4636	61.0 per cent
Labour costs	2356	31.0 per cent
Overheads	1120	14.7 per cent
Net profits	1160	15.3 per cent

A10.7

		£	
(a)	Cost of goods sold	7 600	36.2 per cent
	Gross profit	13 400	63.8 per cent
	Labour costs and expenses	7 800	37.14 per cent
	Staff meals	600	2.86 per cent
	Net profit	5 000	23.8 per cent
(b)	Cost of goods sold	5 960	33.1 per cent
	Gross profit	12 040	66.9 per cent
	Labour costs and expenses	7 250	40.3 per cent
	Staff meals	670	3.7 per cent
	Net profit	4 120	22.9 per cent

A10.8

Flamingo Hotel, Budget 19_ _

Department	Sales budget £	Percentage
Room sales	125 212	53
Restaurant sales	77 963	33
Bar sales	28 350	12
Other sales	4 725	2
Total sales	236 250	100

A10.9

Seagull Hotel, Budget 19_ _

Department	Sales budget £	Percentage
Room sales	232 195	51
Restaurant sales	136 586	30
Bar sales	63 740	14
Other sales	22 764	5
Total sales	455 285	100

A10.10

Pelican Hotel, Labour Costs

	Actual 19_ _		Budget 19_ _	
Department	£	Percentage	£	Percentage
Front office				
Reception	14 756	17	17 480	17
Porterage	6 076	7	7 198	7
Housekeeping	21 700	25	25 707	25
Bars	8 680	10	10 283	10
Restaurant	16 492	19	19 537	19
Kitchen	19 096	22	22 622	22
Totals	86 800	100	102 827	100

Turnover £310 000
Labour costs 28 per cent

Turnover £331 700
Labour cost 31 per cent

A10.11   *Swan Hotel, Labour Costs*

| | Actual 19–– | | Budget 19–– | |
Department	£	Percentage	£	Percentage
Front office				
Reception	11 964	15	14 476	15
Porterage	4 785	6	5 790	6
Housekeeping	21 534	27	26 056	27
Bars	9 570	12	11 580	12
Restaurant	14 356	18	17 371	18
Kitchen	17 546	22	21 231	22
Totals	79 755	100	96 504	100

Turnover   £265 850   Turnover £292 435
Labour costs 30 per cent   Labour costs 33 per cent

A10.12   Room occupancy percentage 70.5 per cent
Bed occupancy percentage 71.9 per cent
Rooms out of service percentage 15.0 per cent
Sleeper loss percentage 16.2 per cent

A10.13 $\dfrac{\text{Actual income}}{\text{Possible income}} = \dfrac{£1419}{£2030} \times \dfrac{100}{1} = 69.9$ per cent

A10.14

		First quarter £	Second quarter £	Third quarter £
(a)	Totals	125 000	127 000	130 000
(b)	Totals	135 000	140 000	145 000
(c)	Totals	5 000	5 500	5 800

Chapter 11

A11.1   *See Chapter 11.*
to
A11.5

Index